KAUKONEN

Detailed Analysis of 8 Classic Songs and Instrumentals

Featuring a Comprehensive Audio Lesson on CD

Cover Photo by Happy Traum

Recorded by Michael Falzarano at Hillside Farm Studios, Darwin, OH

Audio Editor: Ted Orr

Mastered by: Ted Orr and George James at Nevessa Productions, Woodstock, NY

ISBN 0-7935-8176-1

7777 W. BLUEMOUND RD. P.O. BOX 13819 MILWAUKEE, WI 53213

Visit Hal Leonard Online at **www.halleonard.com**

Visit Homespun Tapes on the internet at **http://www.homespuntapes.com**

CD instruction makes it easy! Find the section of the lesson you want with the press of a finger; play that segment over and over until you've mastered it; easily skip over parts you've already mastered—no clumsy rewinding or fast-forwarding to find your spot; listen with the best possible audio fidelity; follow along track-by-track with the book.

THE GUITAR OF JORMA KAUKONEN

Detailed Analysis of 8 Classic Songs and Instrumentals

Featuring a Comprehensive Audio Lesson on CD

Table of Contents

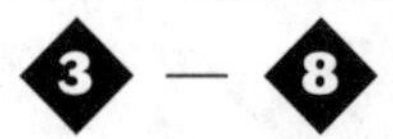

2 Embryonic Journey

Words and Music by Jorma Kaukonen

Drop D Tuning
(1) = E (4) = D
(2) = B (5) = A
(3) = G (6) = D

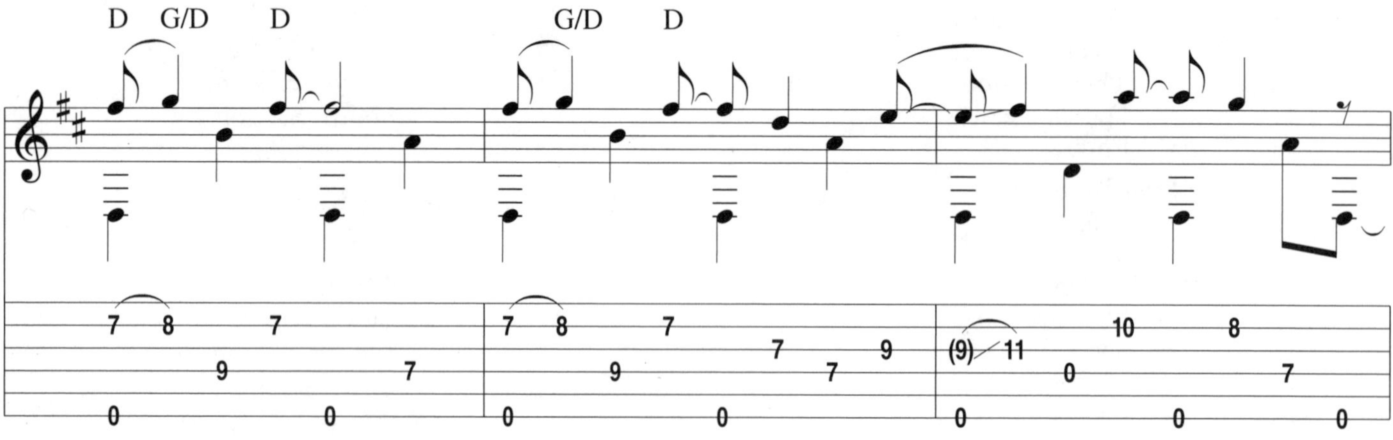

B G
G
F♯m
Em
A
D

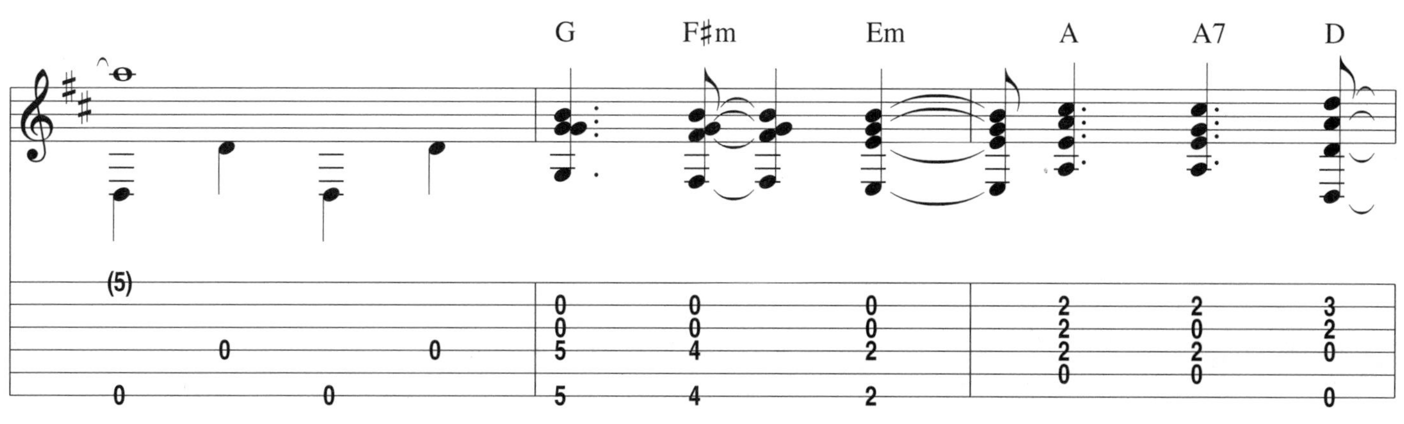
G
F♯m
Em
A
A7
D

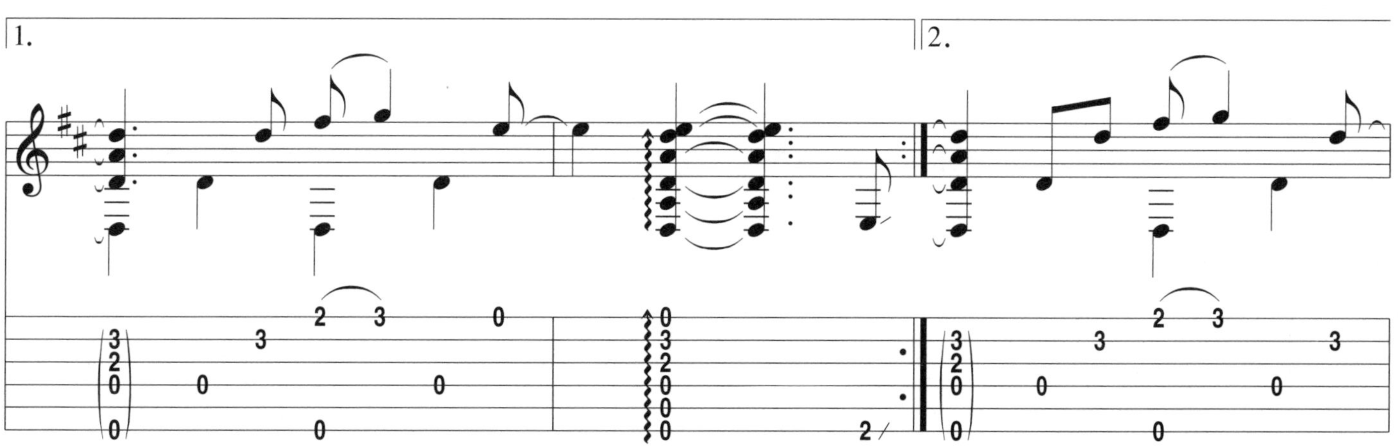
1.
2.

C
To Coda
D
D
D6/9
E♭6/9
D6/9
Dsus
D6/9
Dsus D6/9
Dsus
D6/9
D
G/D
G
A
D

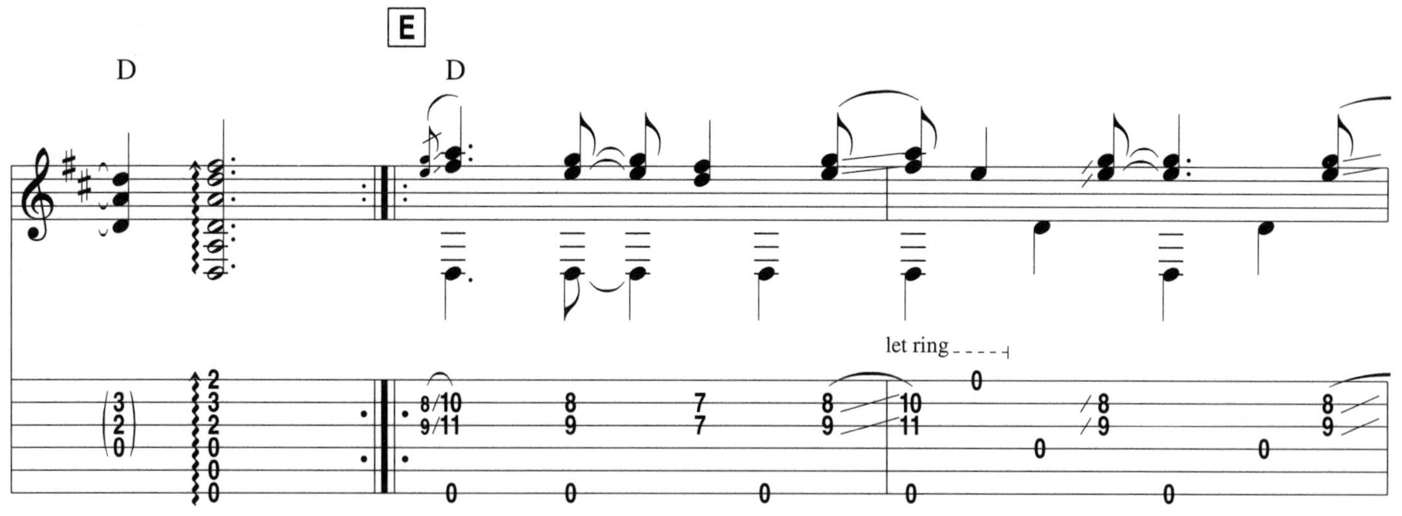
E
D
D
let ring

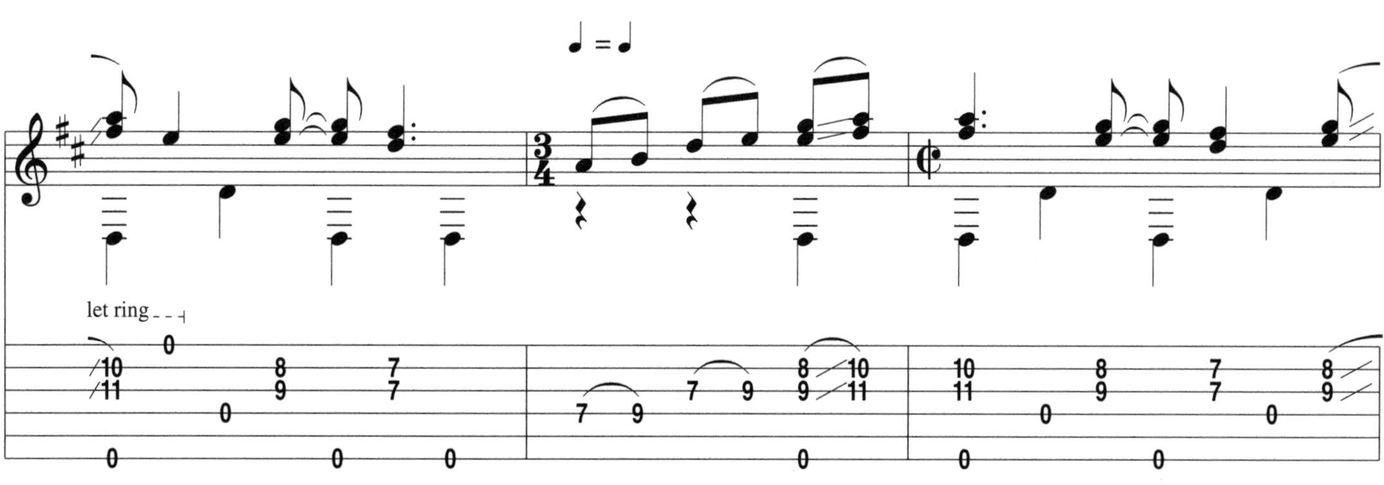
let ring

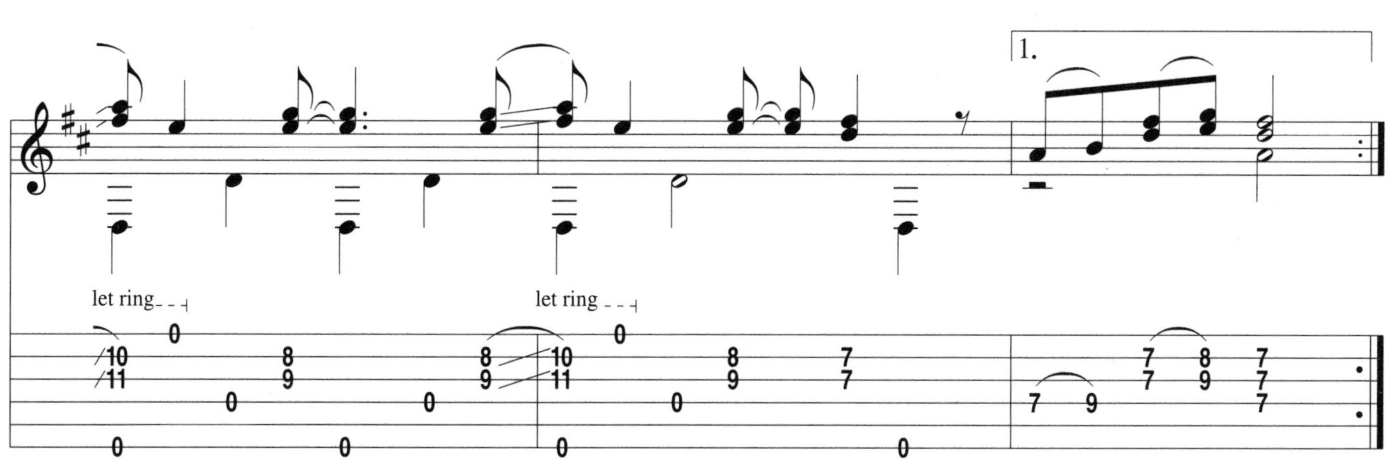
1.
let ring
let ring

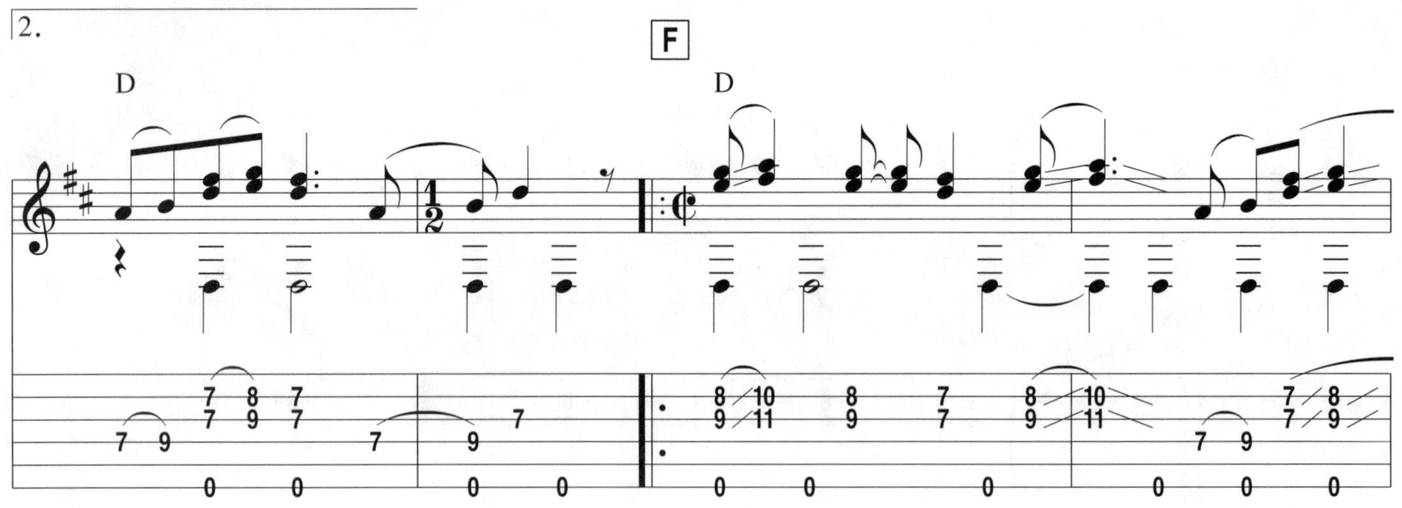
2.
F
D
D

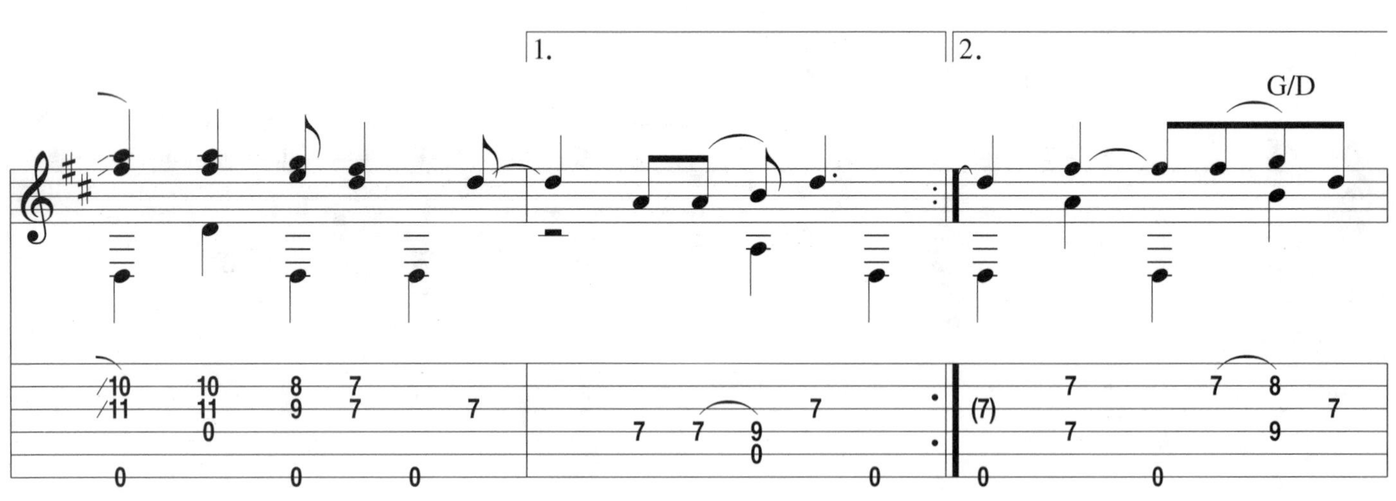
1.
2.
G/D

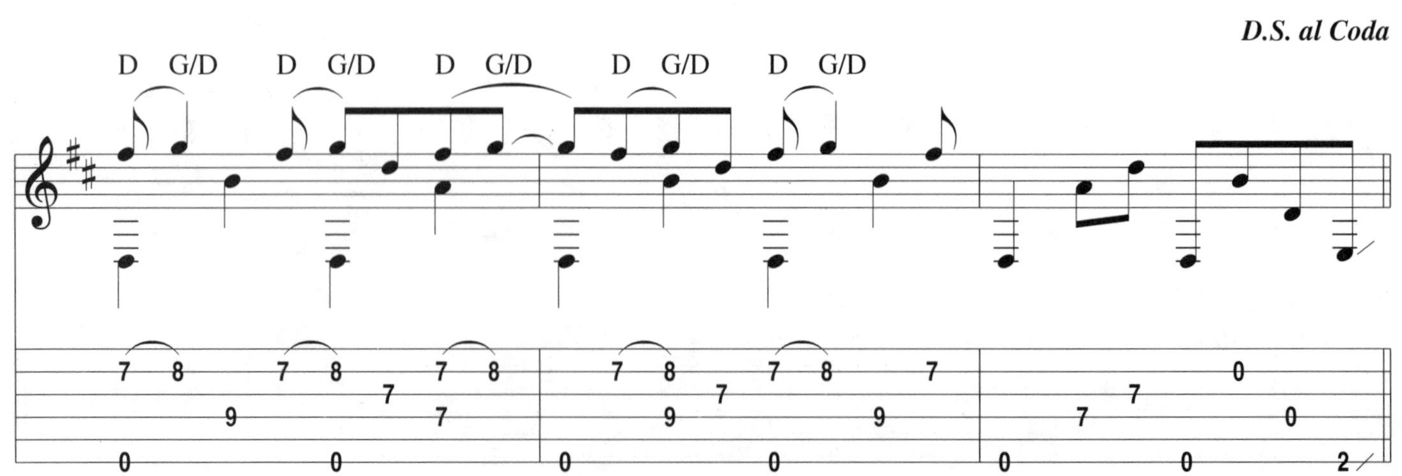
D.S. al Coda
D G/D D G/D D G/D D G/D D G/D

Coda

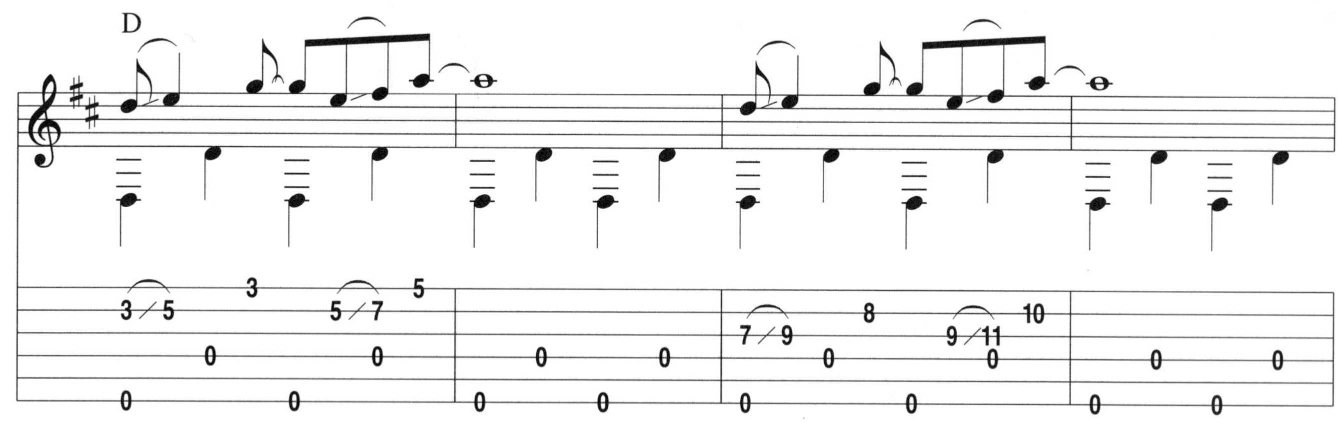

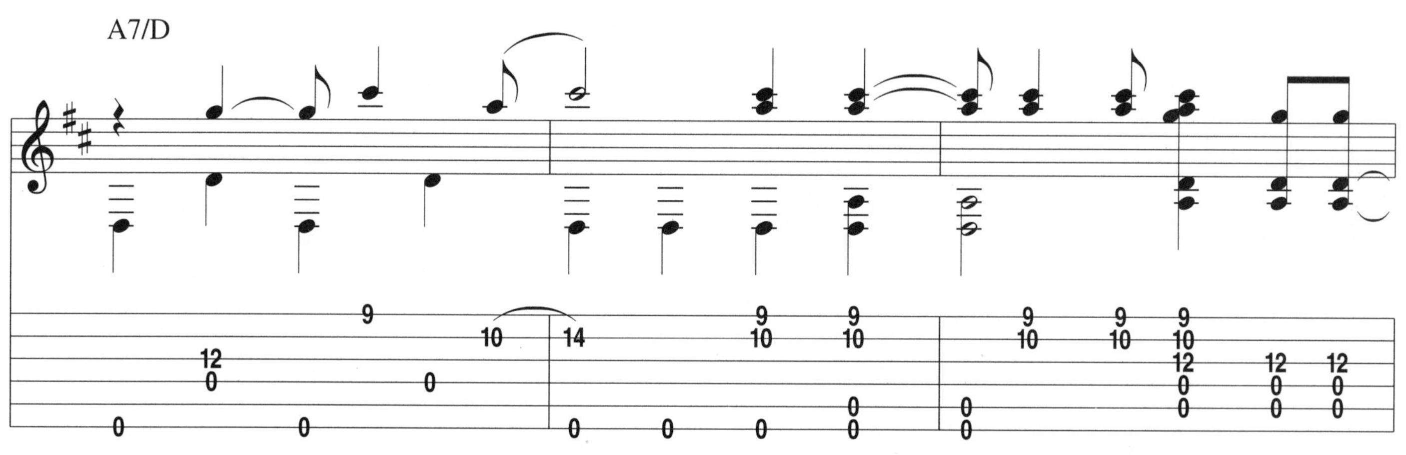

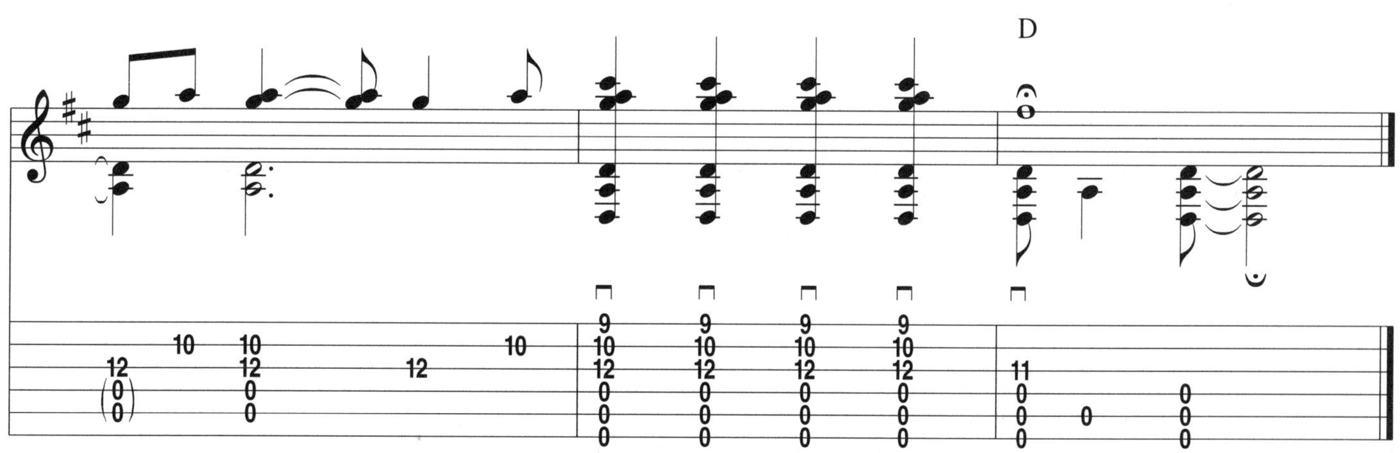

Trial By Fire

10

Words and Music by Jorma Kaukonen

Capo II
Drop D Tuning:
1 = E 4 = D
2 = B 5 = A
3 = G 6 = D

Moderately Fast 𝅗𝅥 = 93

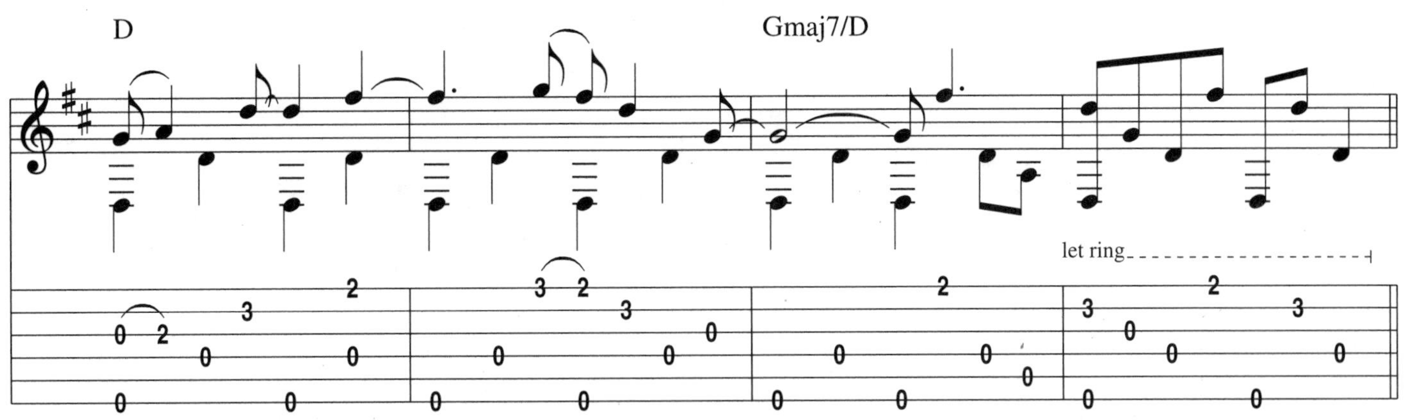
D
Gmaj7/D
let ring

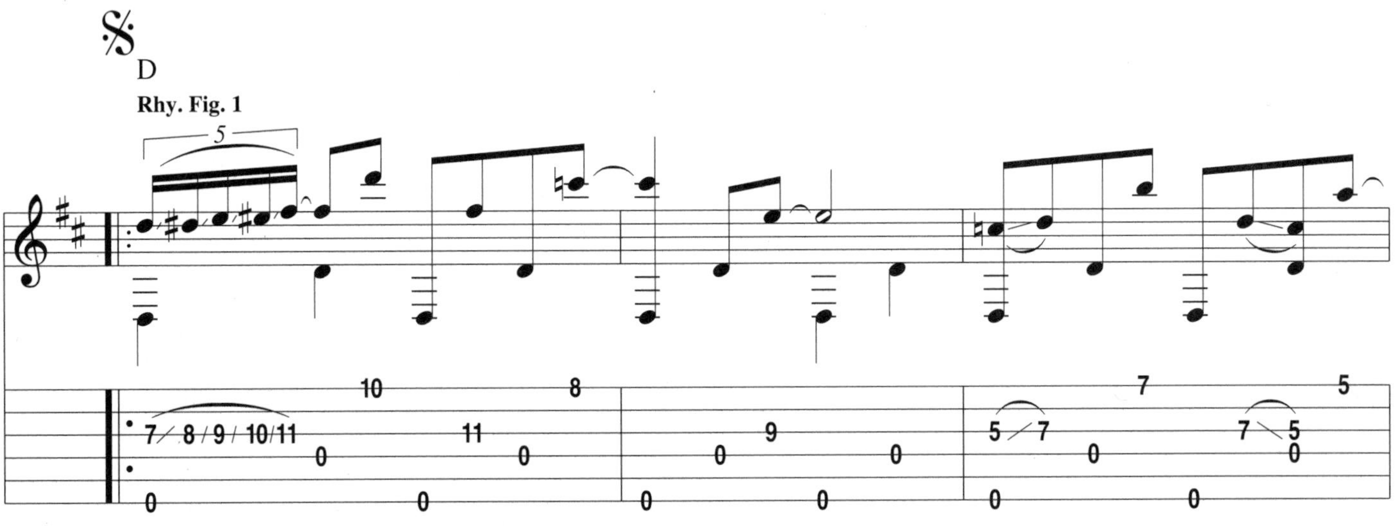
D
Rhy. Fig. 1

1.,2.
3.
Verse
w/ Rhy. Fig. 1, two times
D
D
1. Gon-na move out on the high-way,
2. See Additional Lyrics
End Rhy. Fig. 1
make this mo-ment last. If it clo-ses with a fu-ture,
D
leav-in' out the past. Roll-in' on I'm do-in' fine, said,
"What do you think I see?" A man come beck-on-in', says
G
D
"Bud-dy, come go with me." Well, an en-gine just ain't strong e-nough for
End Rhy. Fig. 1
Rhy. Fig. 2
End Rhy. Fig. 2

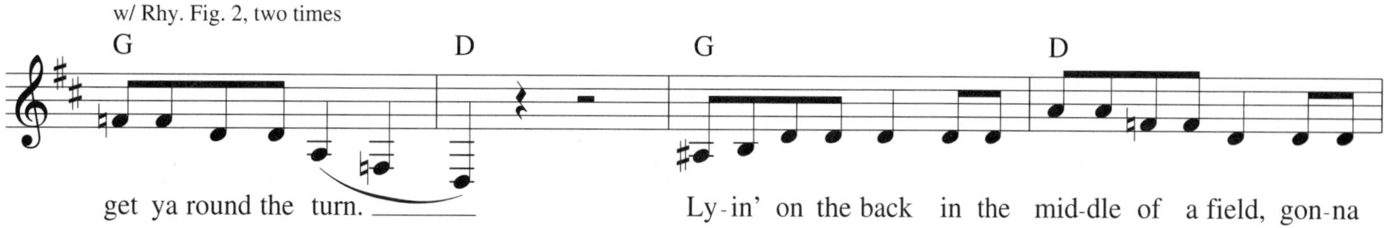
w/ Rhy. Fig. 2, two times
G
D
G
D
get ya round the turn.
Ly-in' on the back in the mid-dle of a field, gon-na

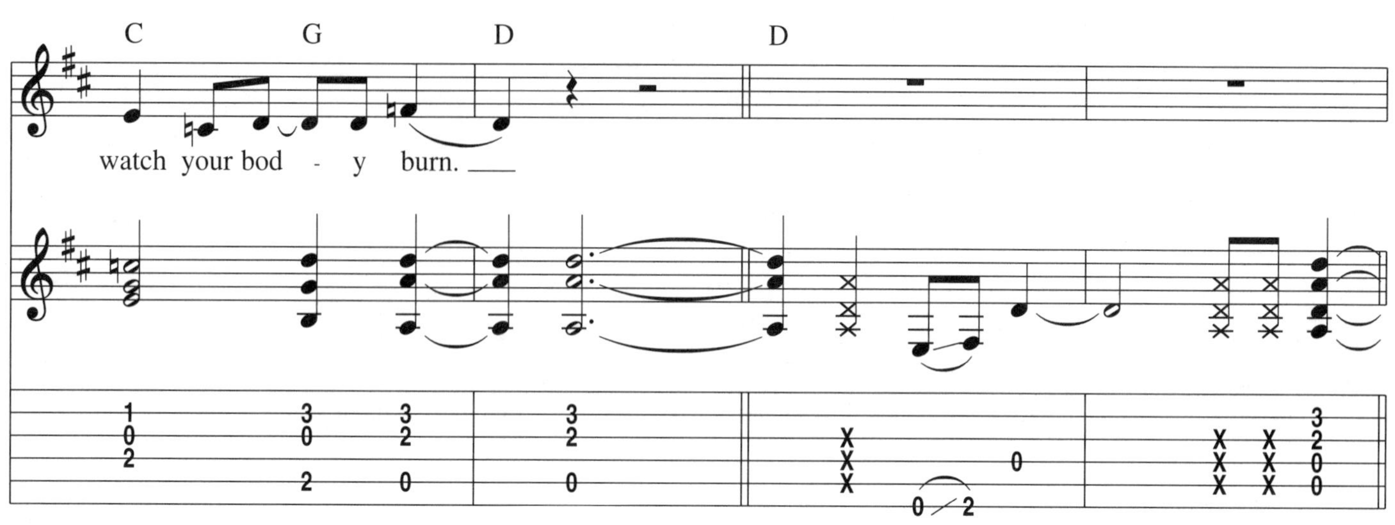
C
G
D
D
watch your bod - y burn.

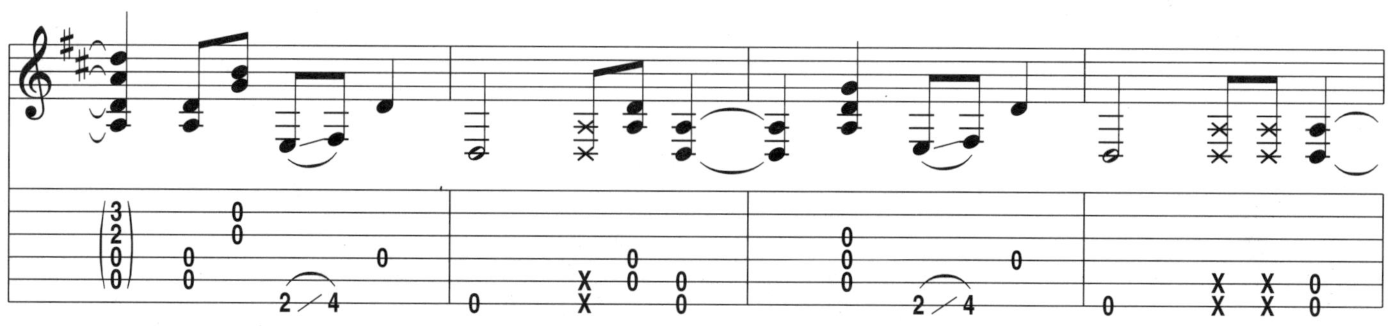

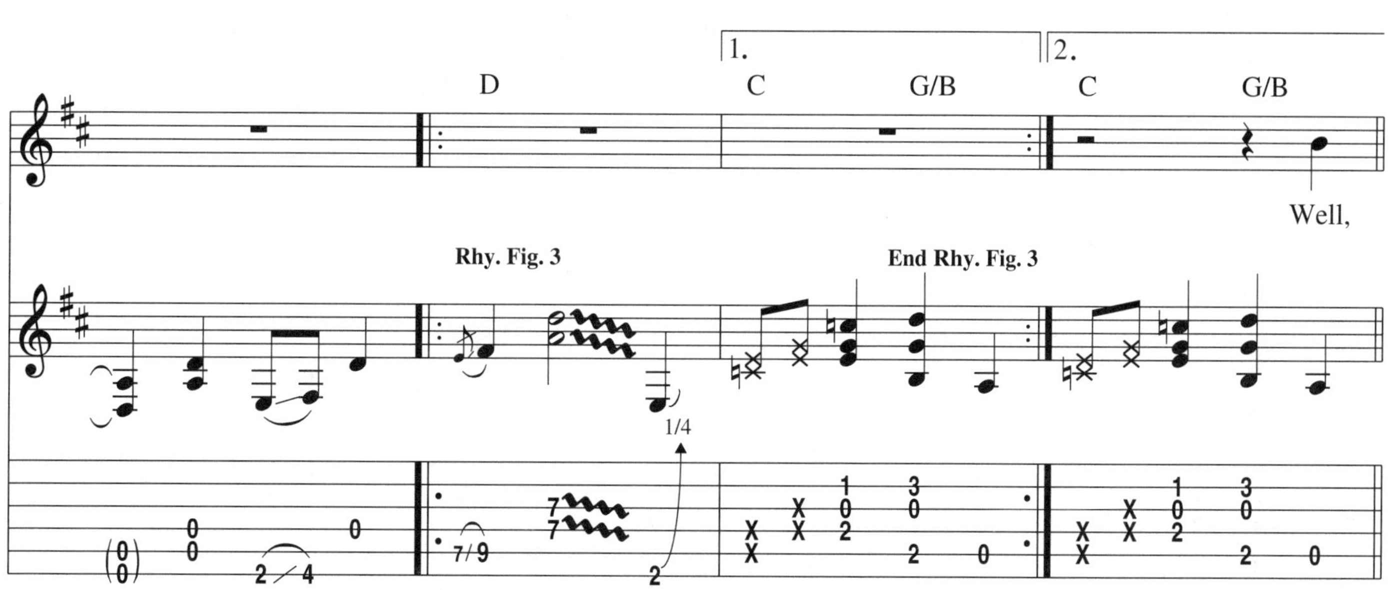
1.
2.
D
C
G/B
C
G/B
Well,
Rhy. Fig. 3
End Rhy. Fig. 3
1/4

Chorus

w/ Rhy. Fig. 3, 8 times
D
C
G/B
D
C
G/B
don't try and tell me just who I am, Lord, you don't ___ know your - self.

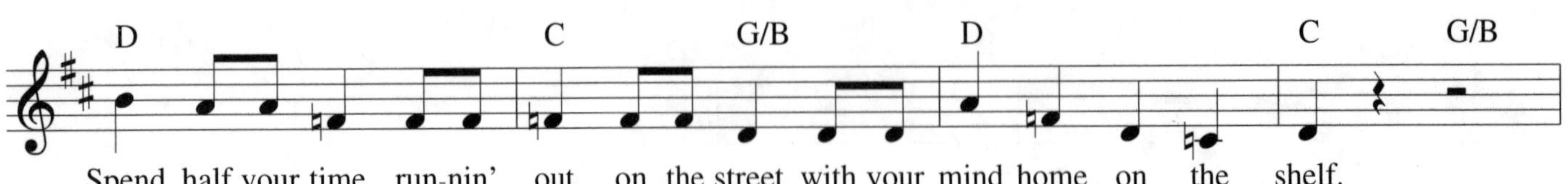
D
C
G/B
D
C
G/B
Spend half your time run-nin' out on the street with your mind home on the shelf.

D
C
G/B
D
C
G/B
Look-in' at me with your eyes full of fire, like you'd ra-ther be see-in' me dead.

To Coda
D
C
G/B
D
C
G/B
Ly - in' on the floor with a hole in my face and a ten gauge shot - gun at my head.

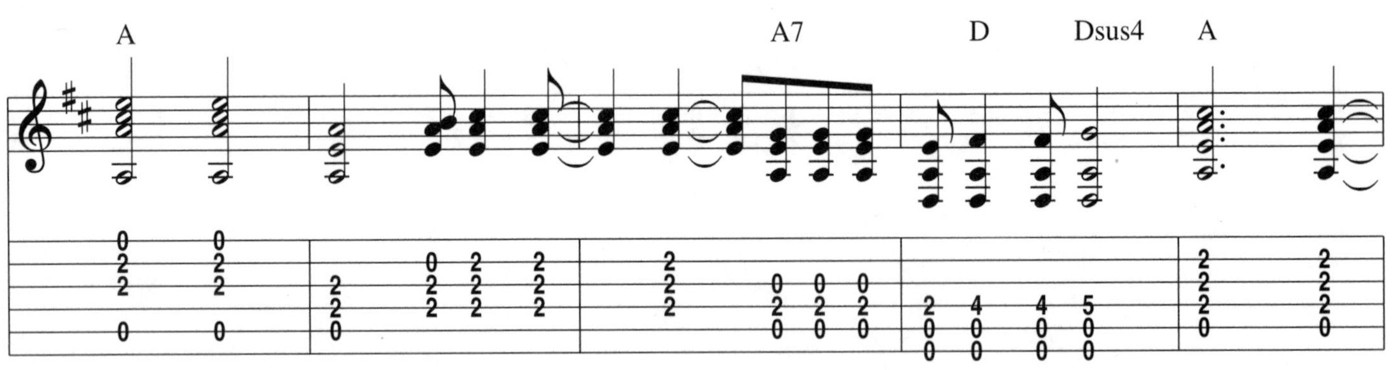
A
A7
D
Dsus4
A

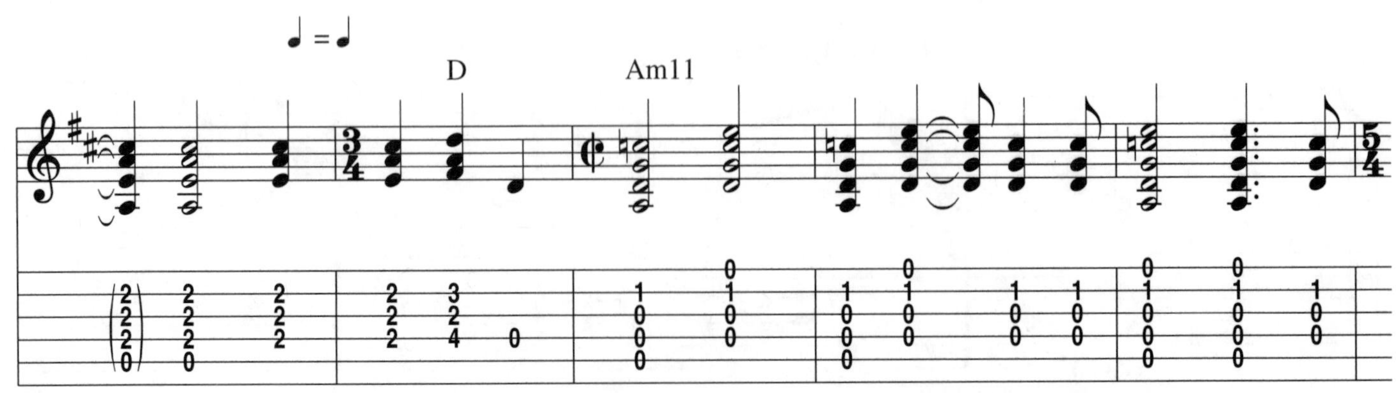
D
Am11

Am11
D
1/2
1.
2.
w/ Rhy. Fig. 2,
3 times simile
6
C
G/B
D
D.S. al Coda
play 3 times

Coda

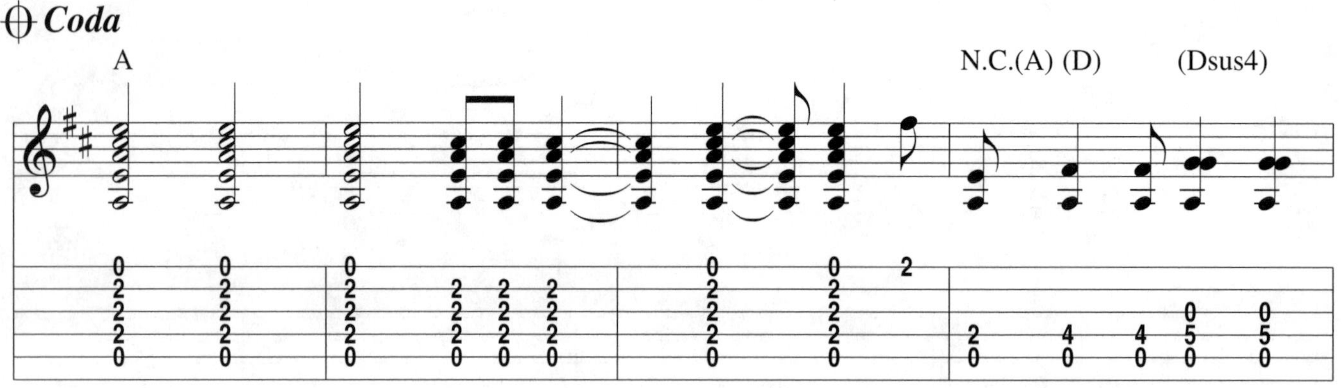

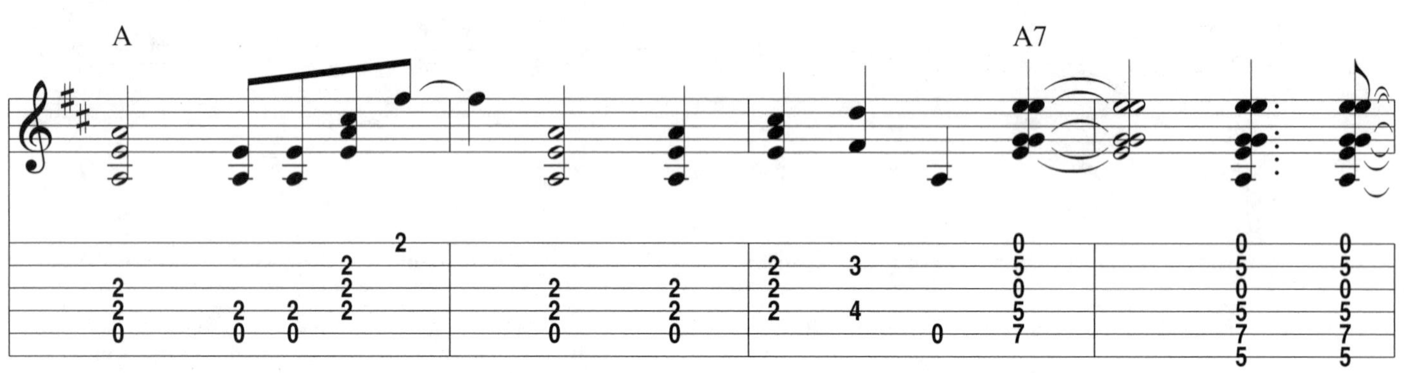

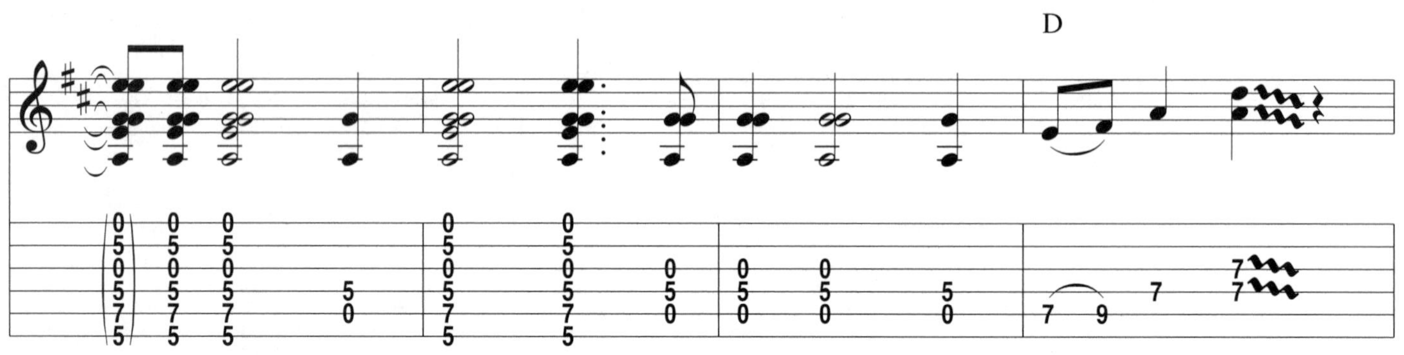

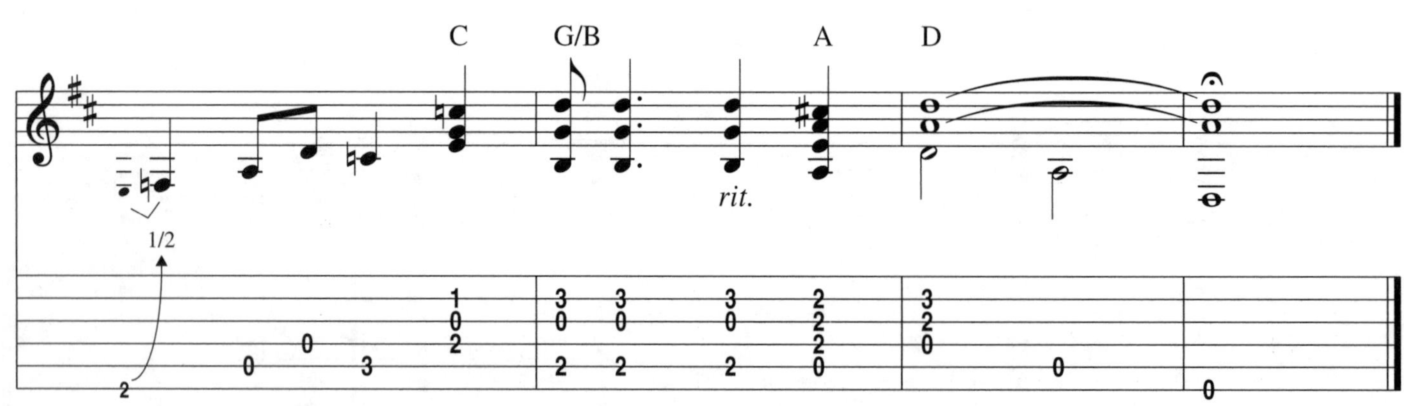

Additional Lyrics

You can lead me here, but I won't tell
The things I know about you I know so well.
Will ya smile at me, try to set me free?
Keep me wonderin' what the future may be?

Oh, rollin' on, won't be long.
I won't leave it 'til I sing this song.

(repeat chorus)

16 Watch The North Wind Rise

Words and Music by Jorma Kaukonen

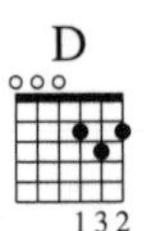

Capo IV
Drop D Tuning:
① = E ④ = D
② = B ⑤ = A
③ = G ⑥ = D

Moderately Fast 𝅗𝅥 = 100

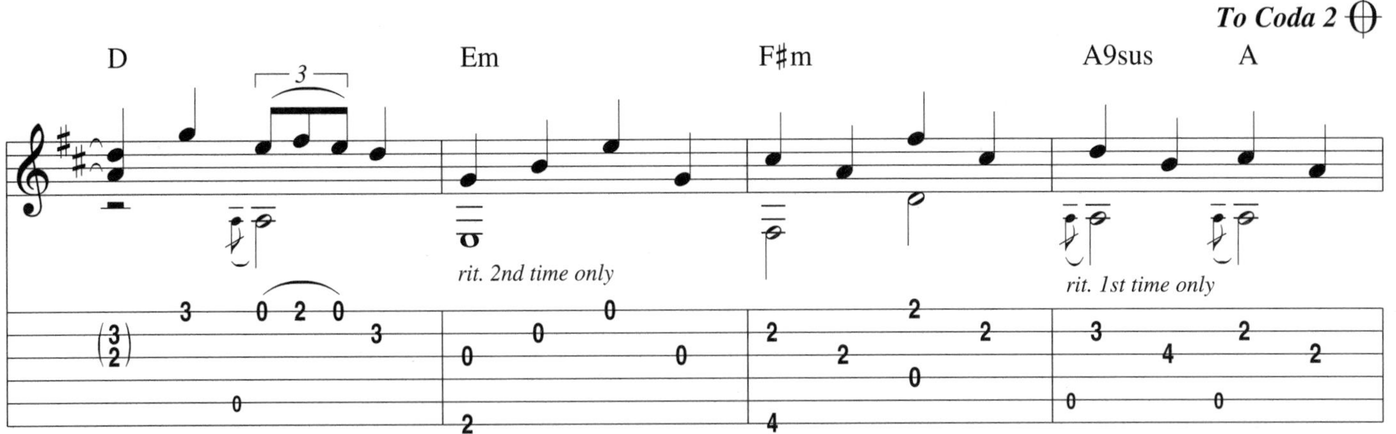
To Coda 2
D
Em
F♯m
A9sus
A
rit. 2nd time only
rit. 1st time only

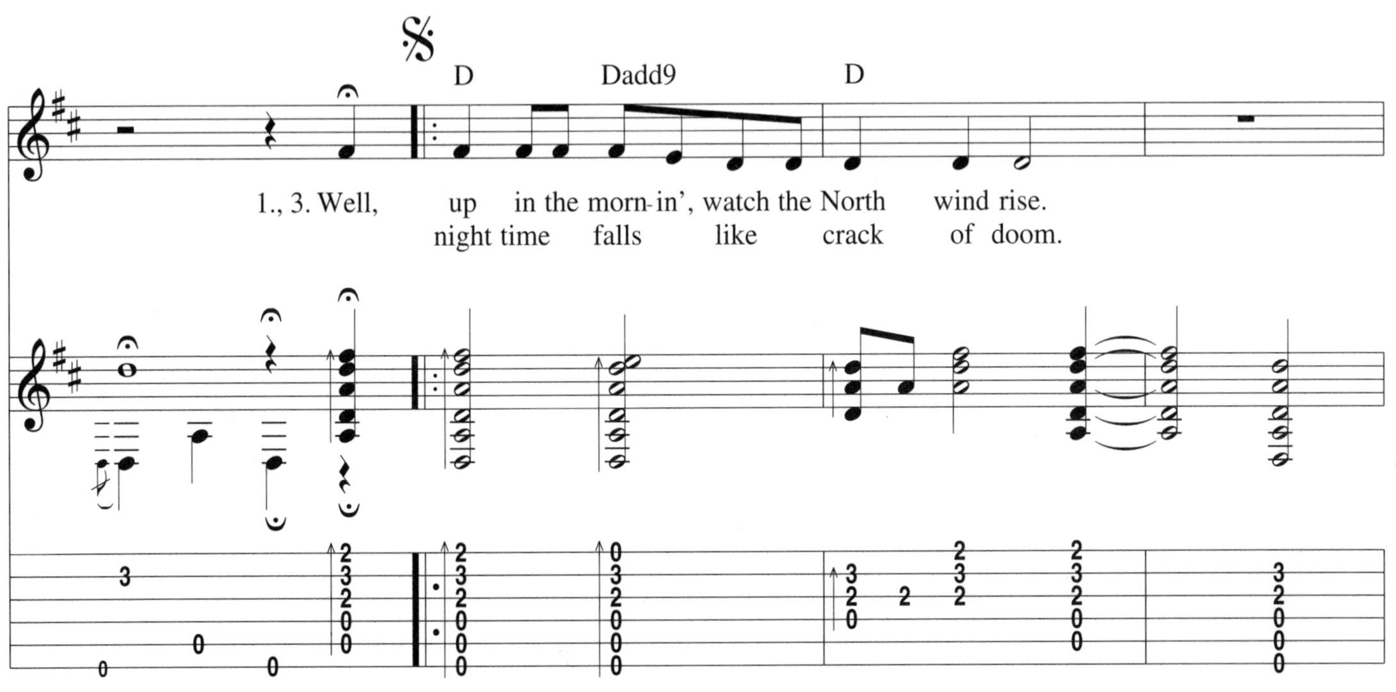
D
Dadd9
D
1., 3. Well, up in the morn-in', watch the North wind rise.
night time falls like crack of doom.

A/D
D
Bring-in' fire down from the skies.
Fills the sky with a shin - in' moon.

A D
Hey, we've got a long way to go.
Sil - ver siren has got to please.

A D
Keep on lov-in' me, make it slow.
Feel-in' your lov-in', down on my knees.

Chorus

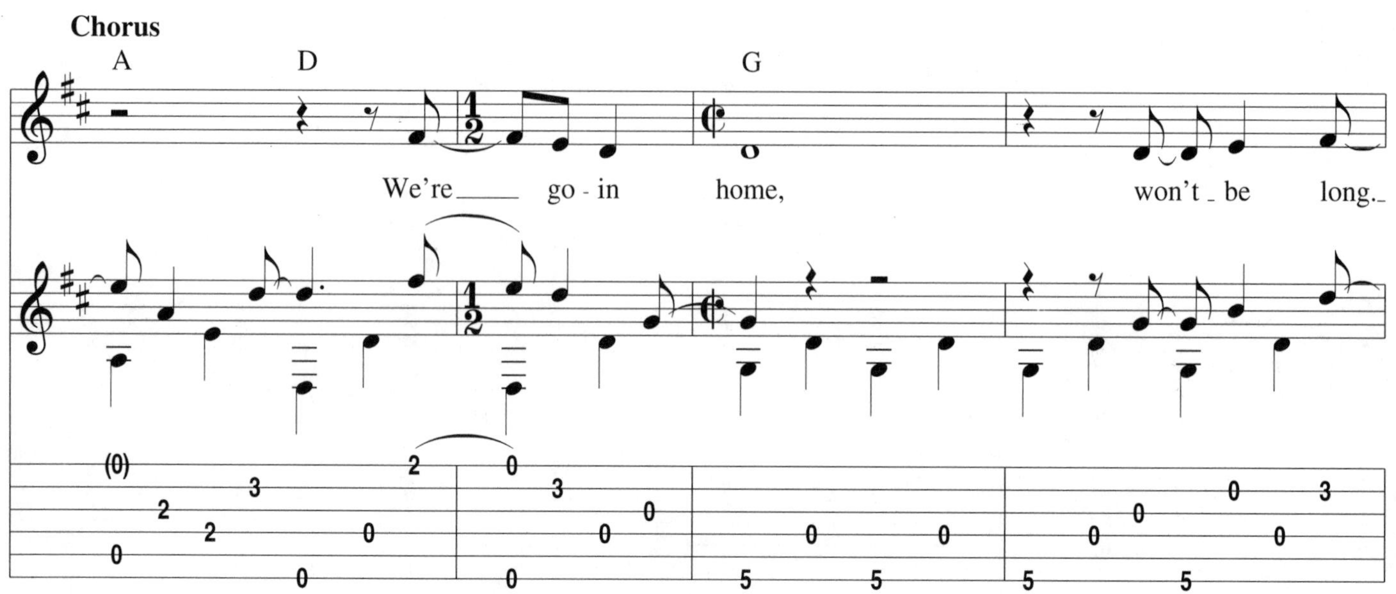
A D G
We're go - in home, won't be long.

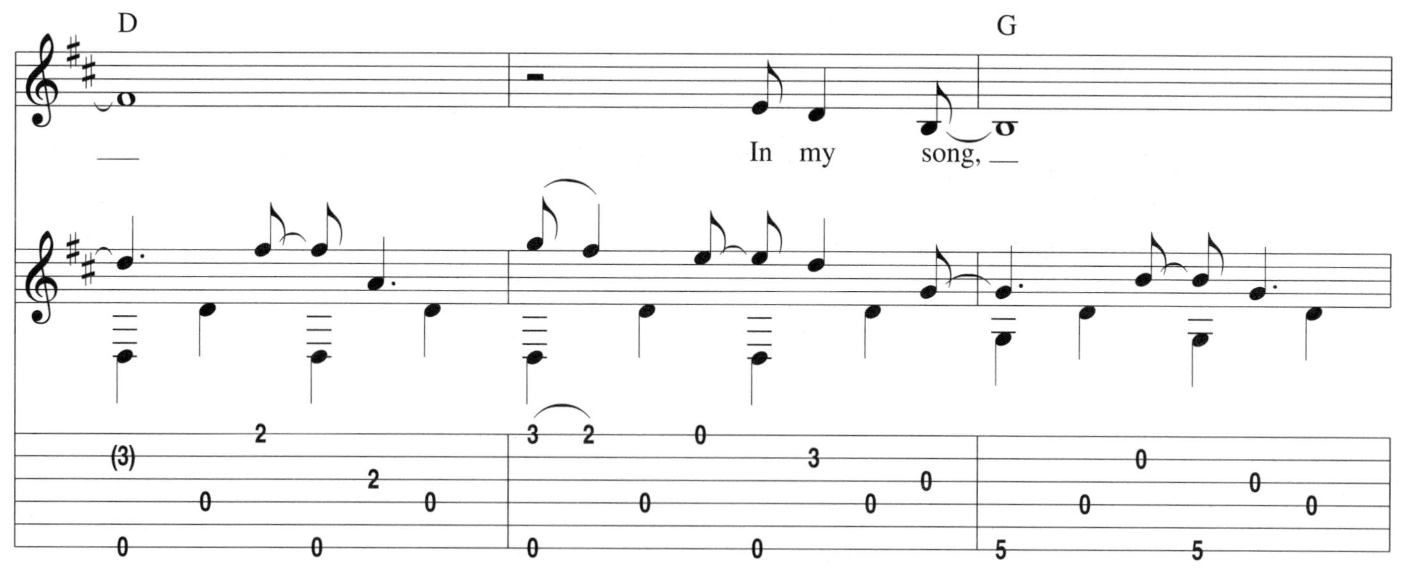
D
G
In my song,
(3)

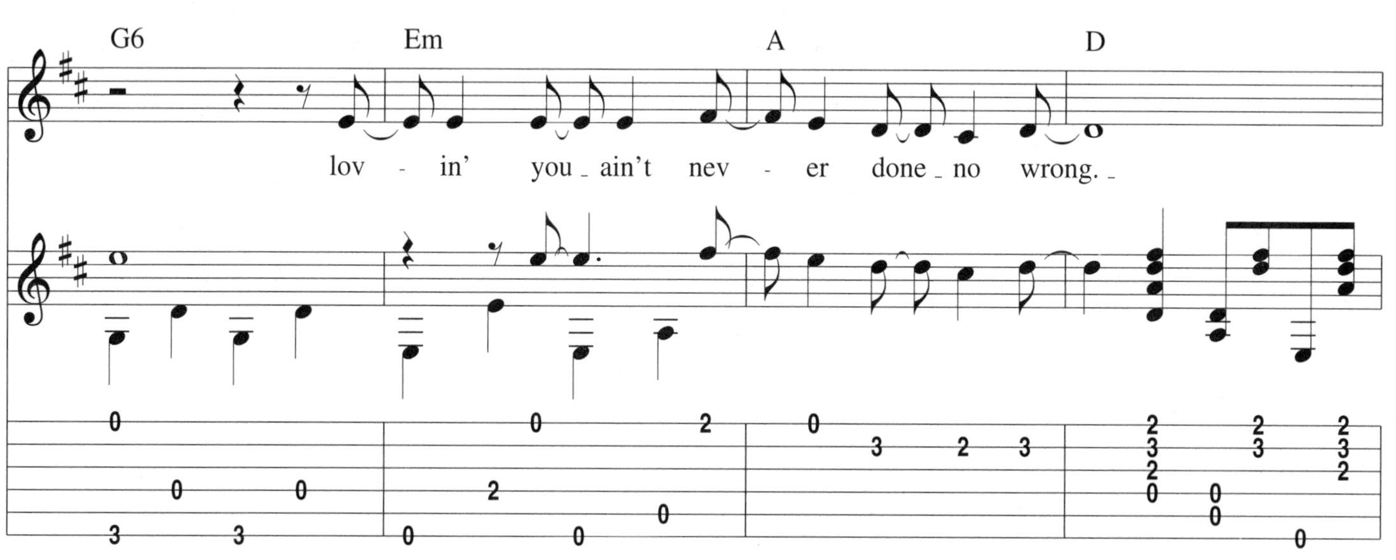
G6
Em
A
D
lov - in' you ain't nev - er done no wrong.

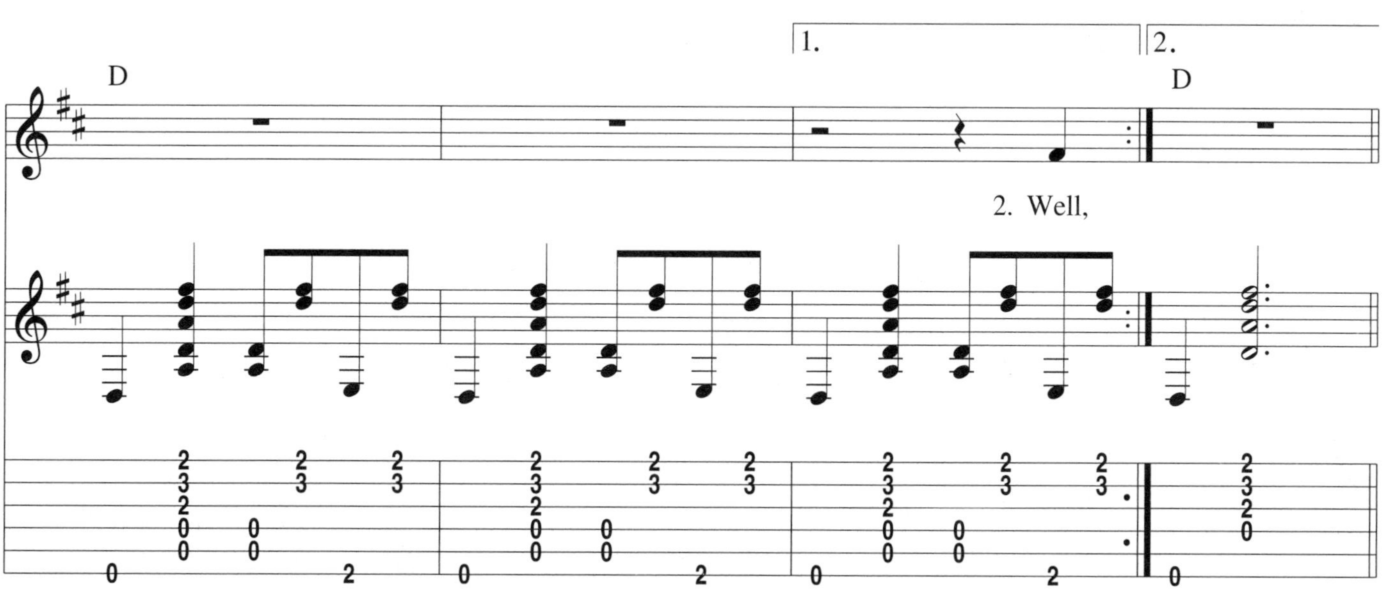
D
1.
2.
D
2. Well,

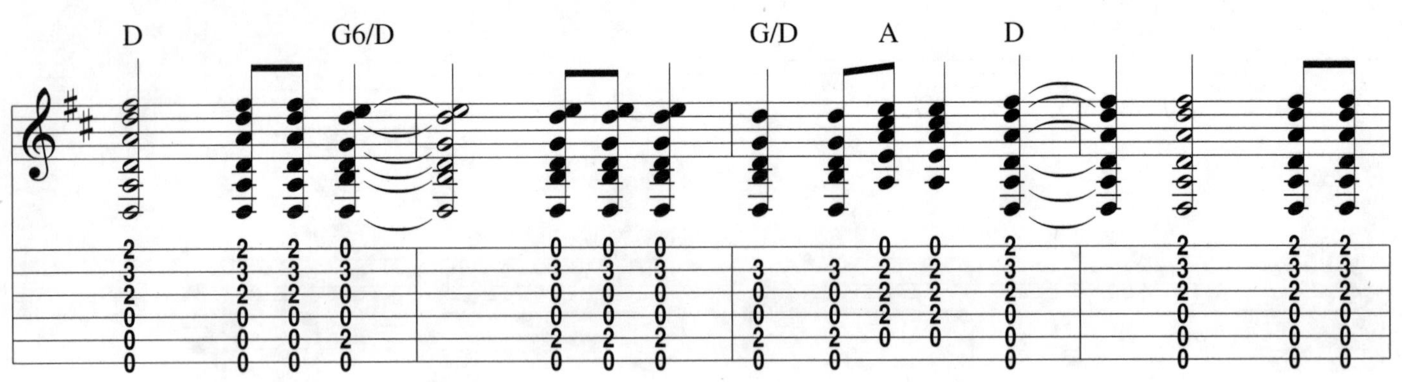
D
G6/D
G/D
A
D

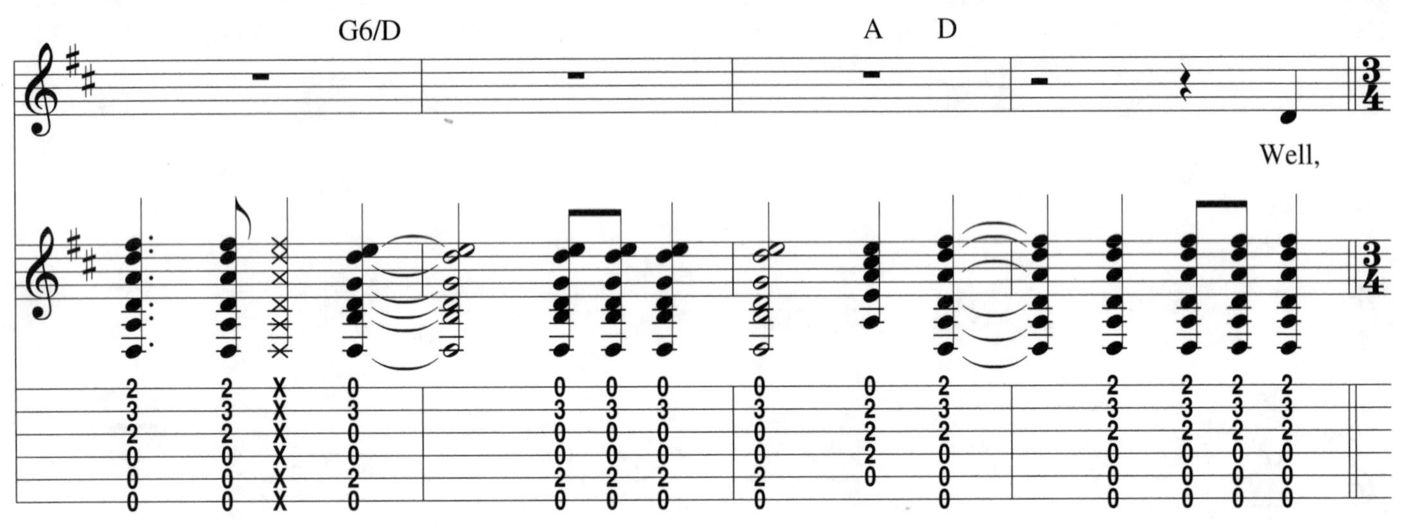
G6/D
A
D
Well,

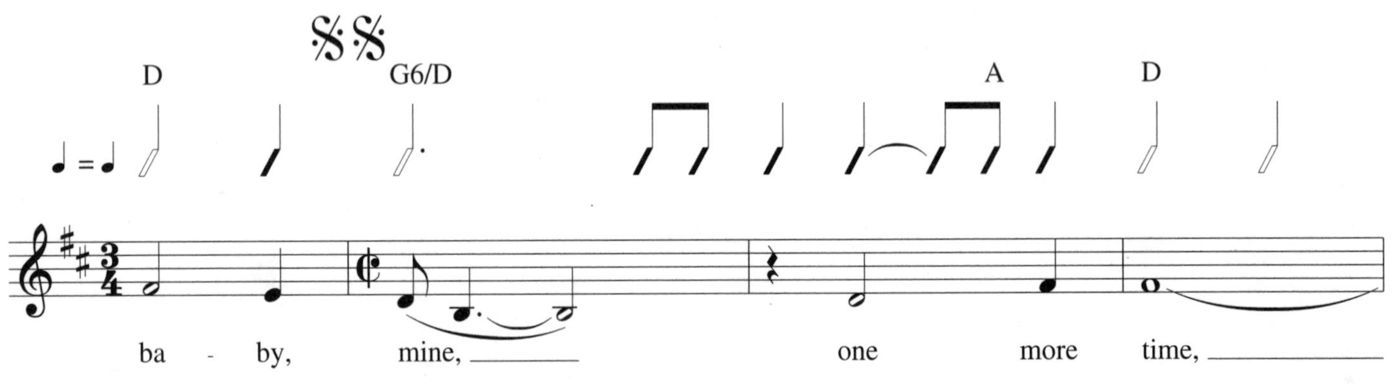
D
G6/D
A
D
ba - by, mine,
one more time,

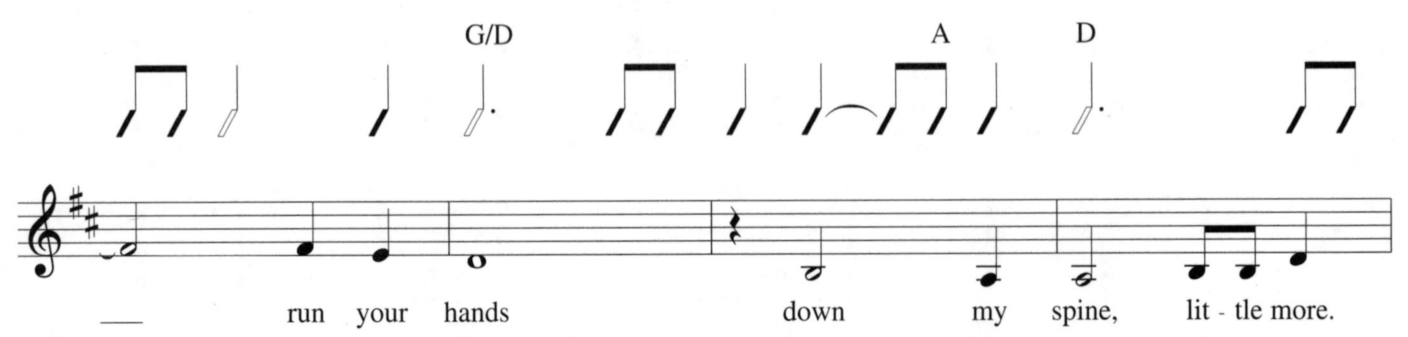
G/D
A
D
run your hands down my spine, lit - tle more.

G/D
A
D
Well, if you say it's time to go,

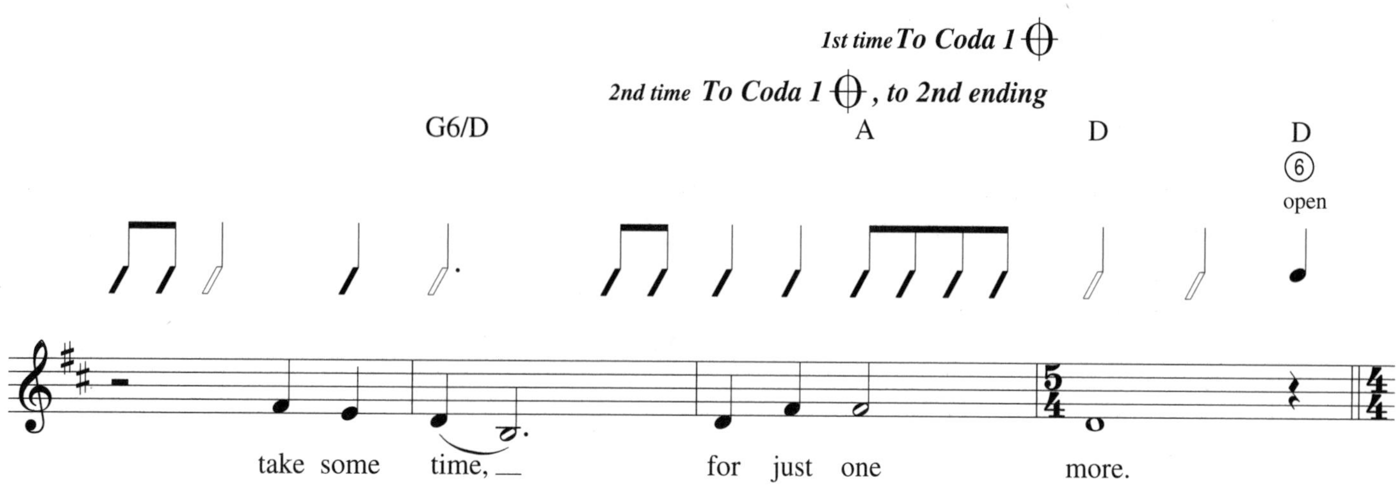
1st time To Coda 1
2nd time To Coda 1, to 2nd ending
G6/D
A
D
D
6
open
take some time, for just one more.

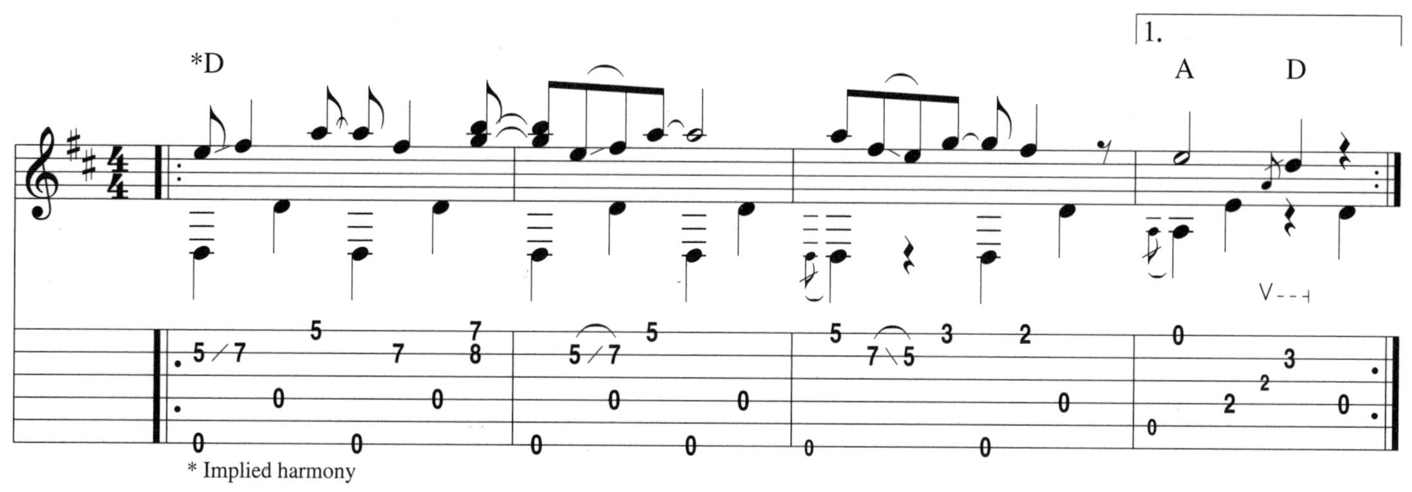
1.
*D
A
D
* Implied harmony

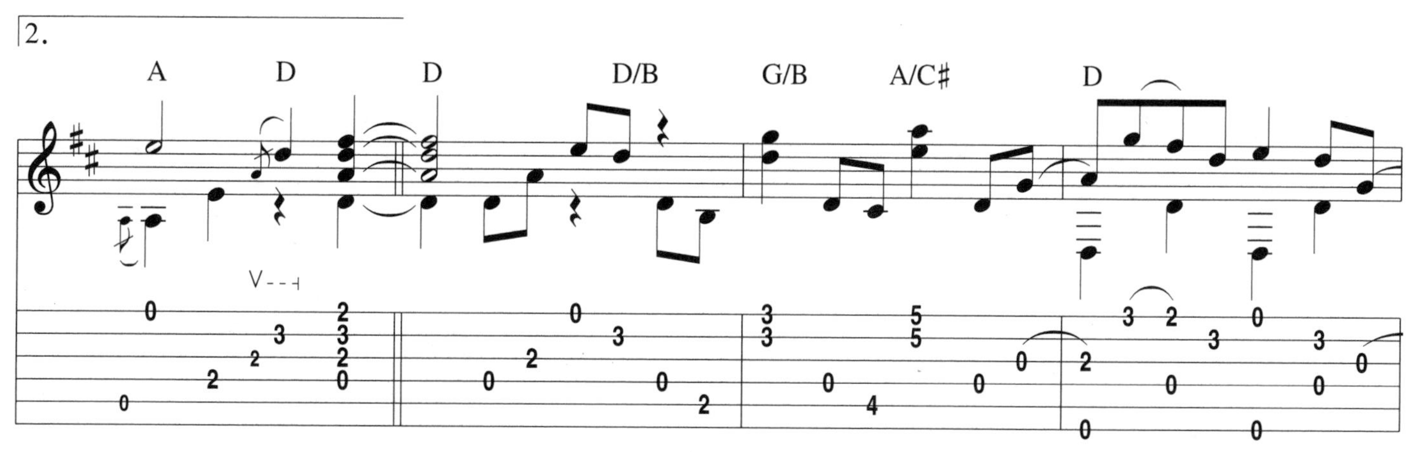
2.
A
D
D
D/B
G/B
A/C♯
D

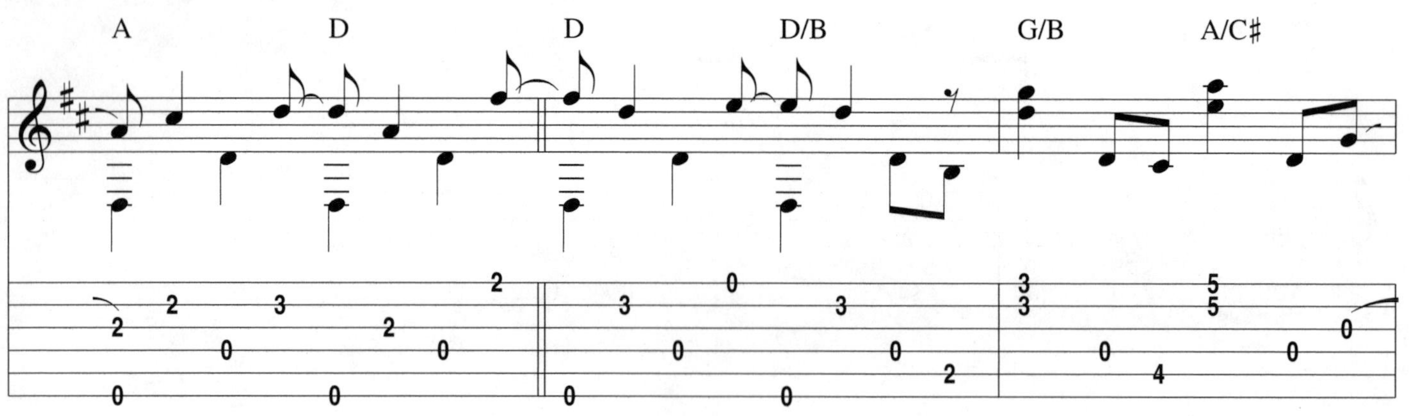
A
D
D
D/B
G/B
A/C♯

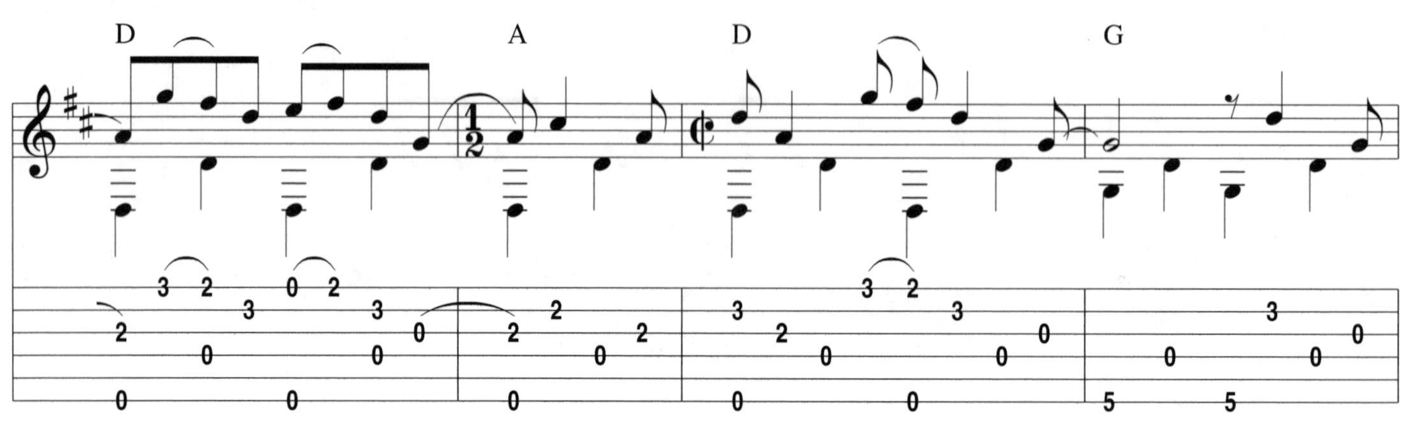
D
A
D
G

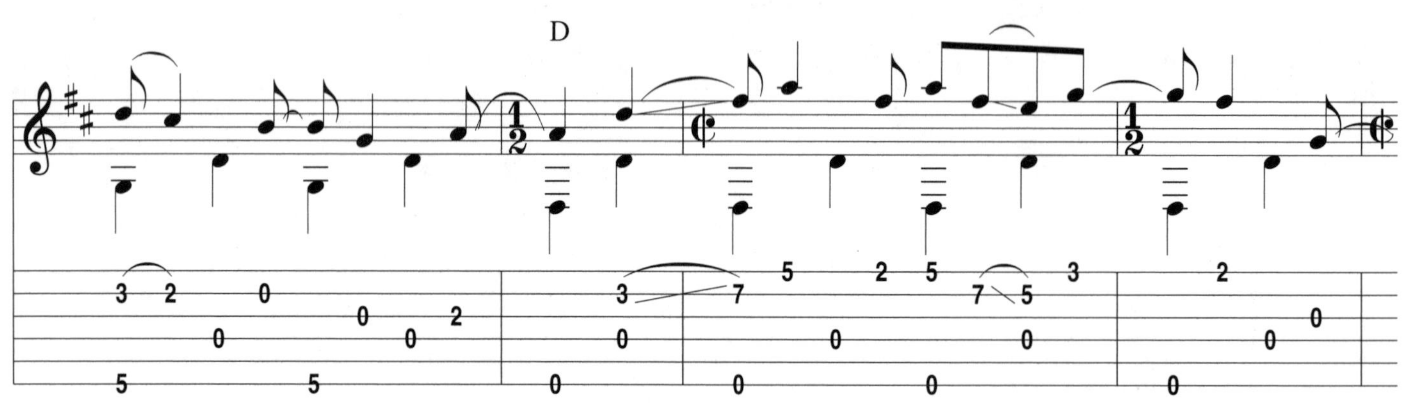
D

G
Em
A

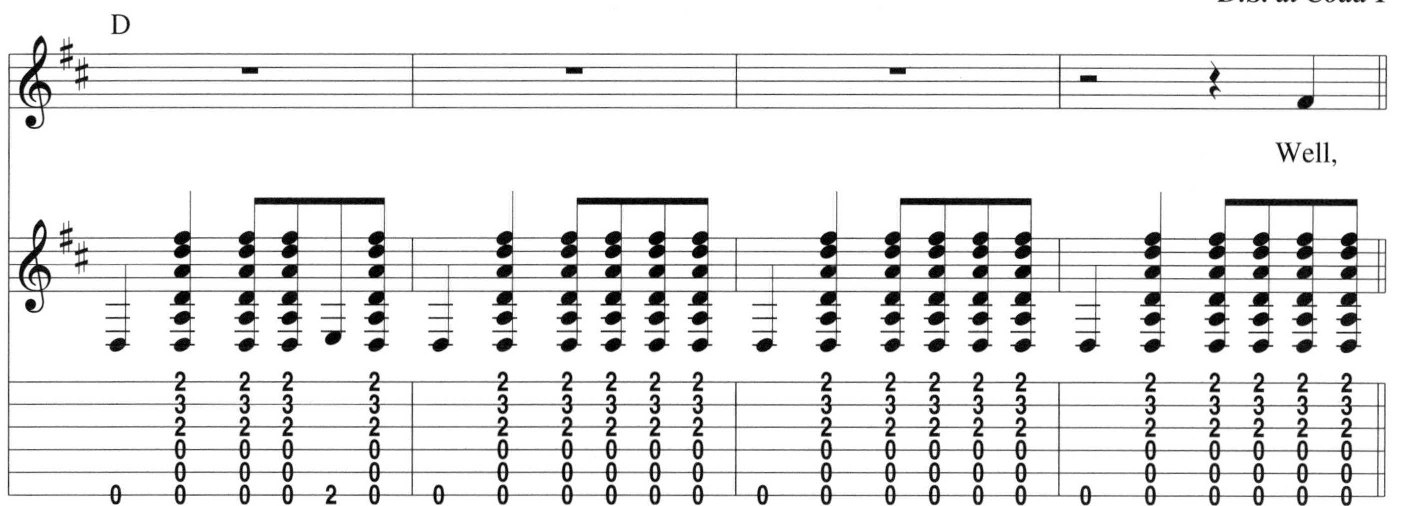
D.S. al Coda 1
D
Well,

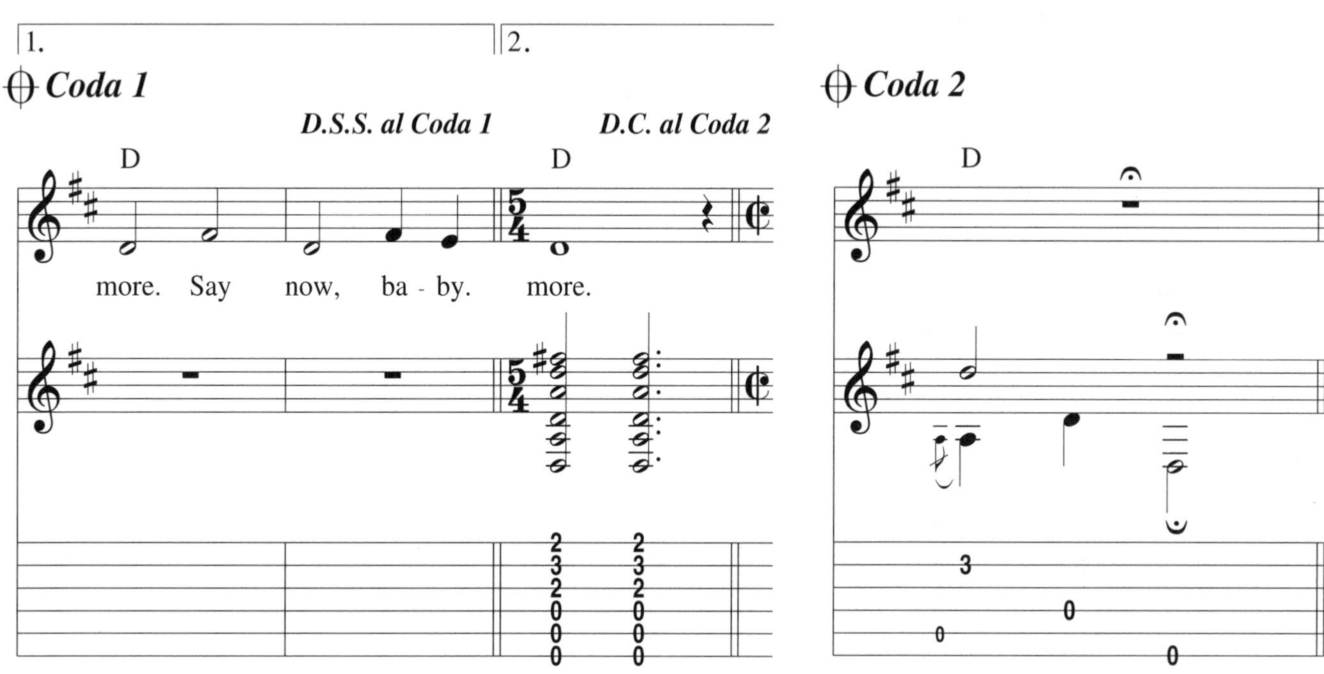
1.
2.
Coda 1
D.S.S. al Coda 1
D.C. al Coda 2
D
more. Say now, ba - by. more.
Coda 2

23

I See The Light

24 — 30

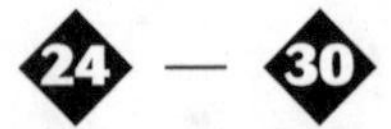

Words and Music by Jorma Kaukonen

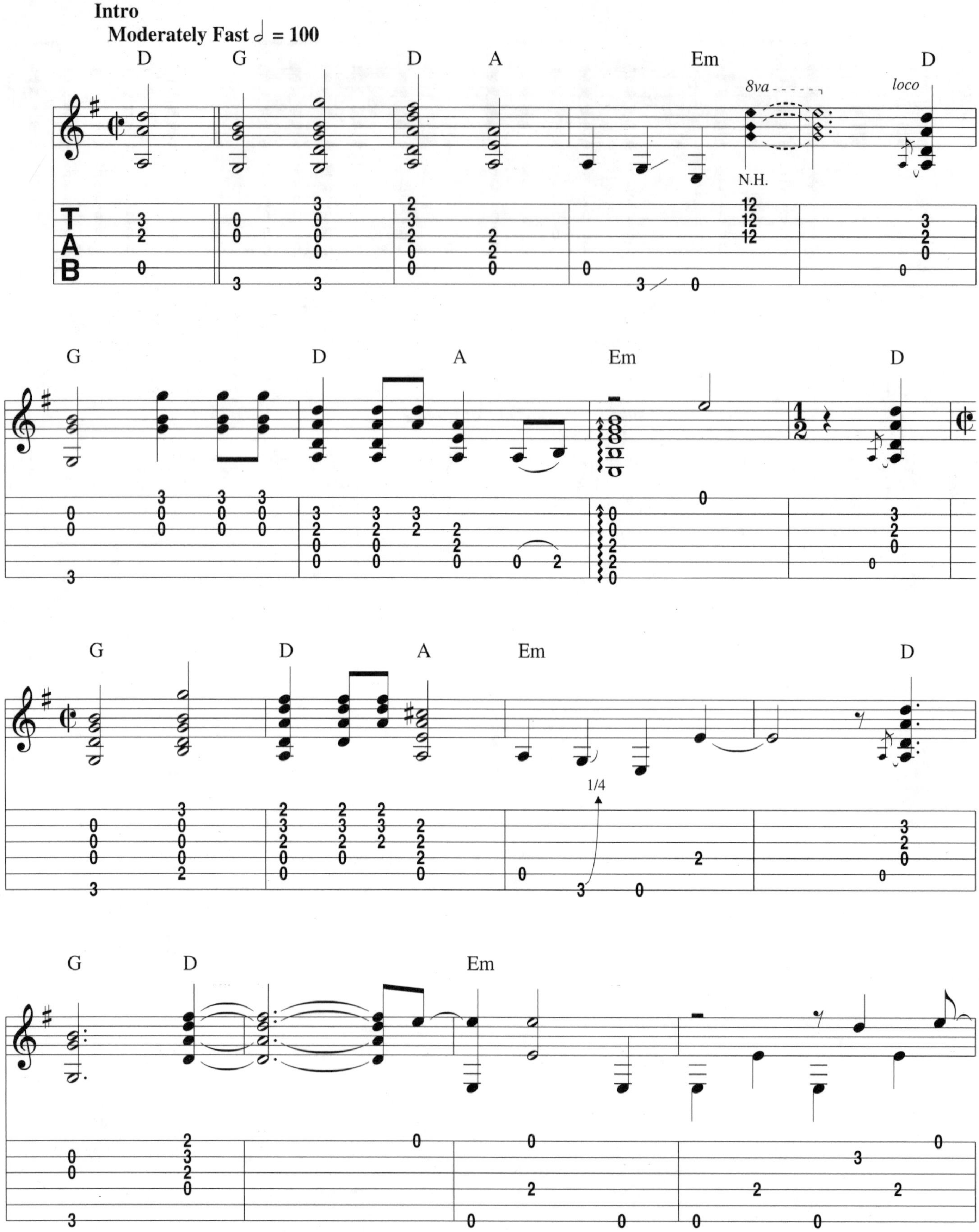

Intro
Moderately Fast 𝅗𝅥 = 100
D G D A Em D
8va
loco
N.H.
T
A
B
G D A Em D
G D A Em D
1/4
G D Em

Em

Em
Em
1. Well, (4.)in this world I'm
2., 3. See Additional Lyrics

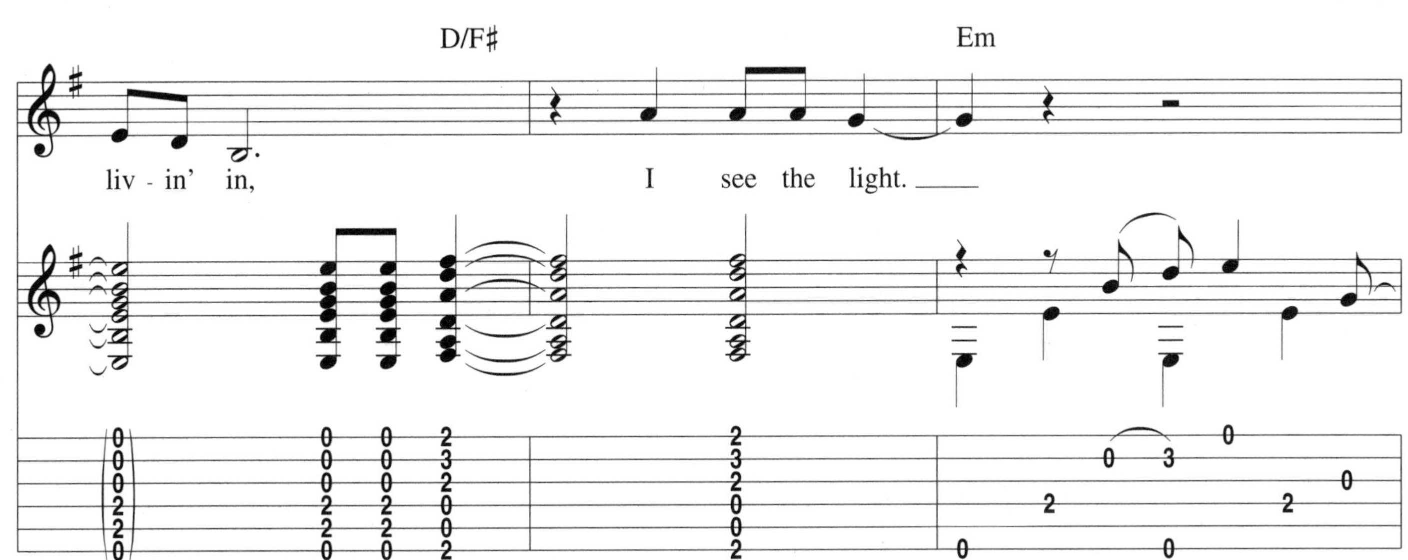
D/F#
Em
liv - in' in,
I see the light.

Em
D
*Our sins are gone and now I know, said, "What is wrong
*Leave this line out of Verse 4

Em
D
and right?" Feel - in' us to - geth - er child,
*Percussive R.H. slap

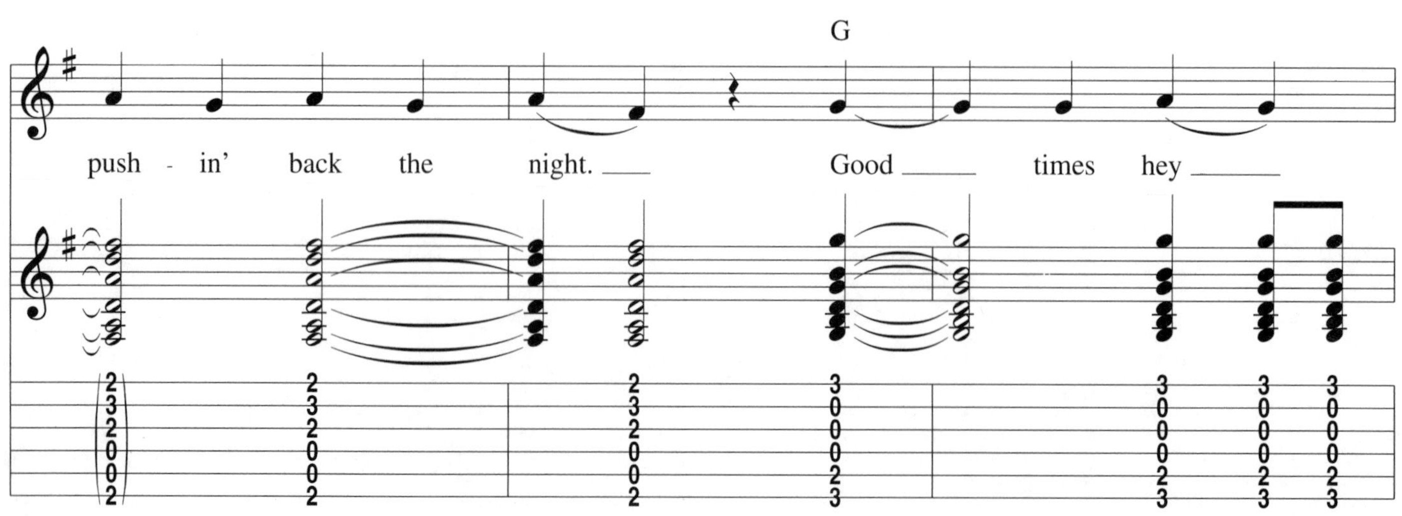
G
push - in' back the night. Good times hey

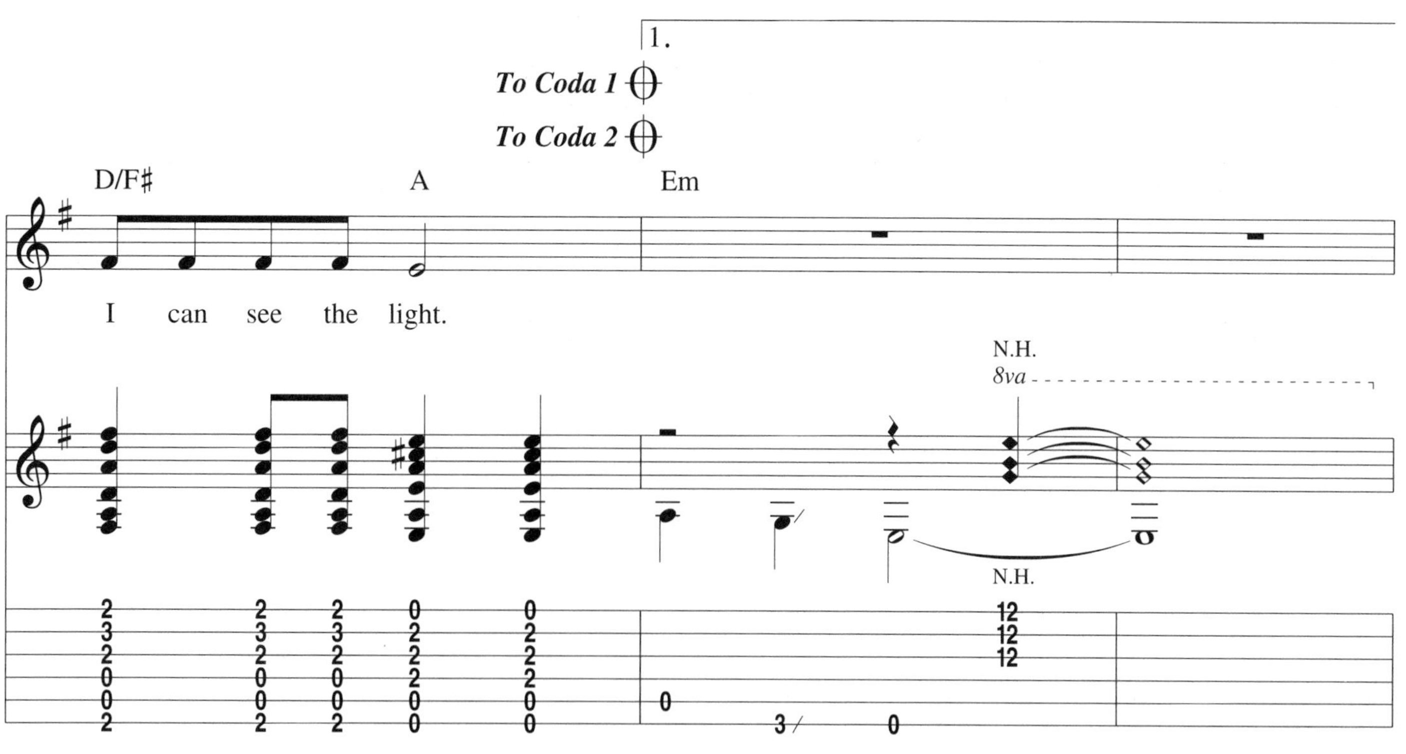
1.
To Coda 1
To Coda 2
D/F♯
A
Em
I can see the light.
N.H.
8va
N.H.

loco
2.

Em
D

Em
D

Em
D

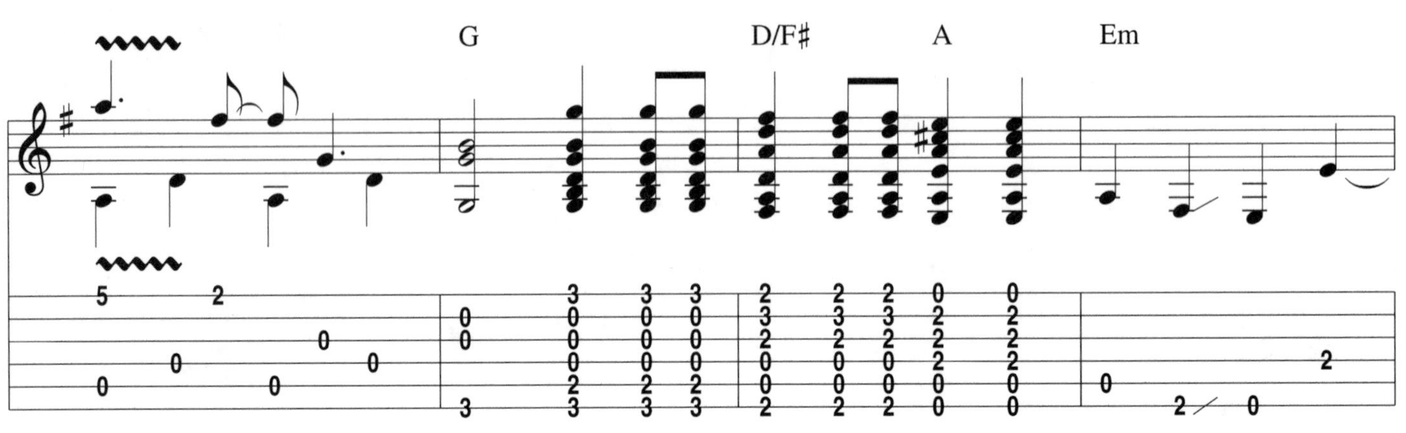
G
D/F♯
A
Em

Em

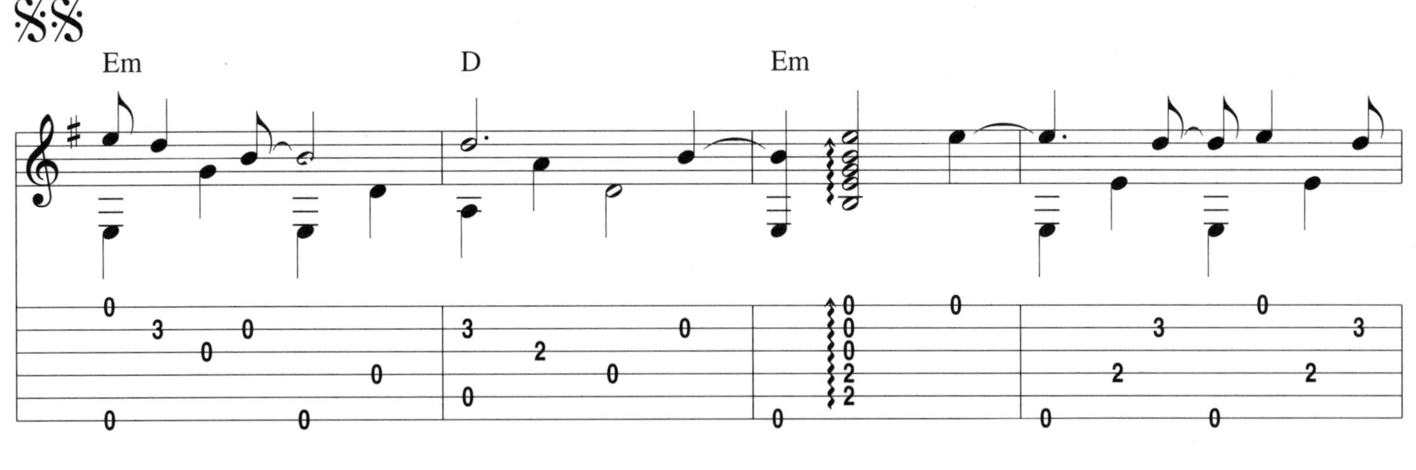

2nd time, D.S. al Coda 2
(repeat 1st Verse Lyrics)
D.S. al Coda 1

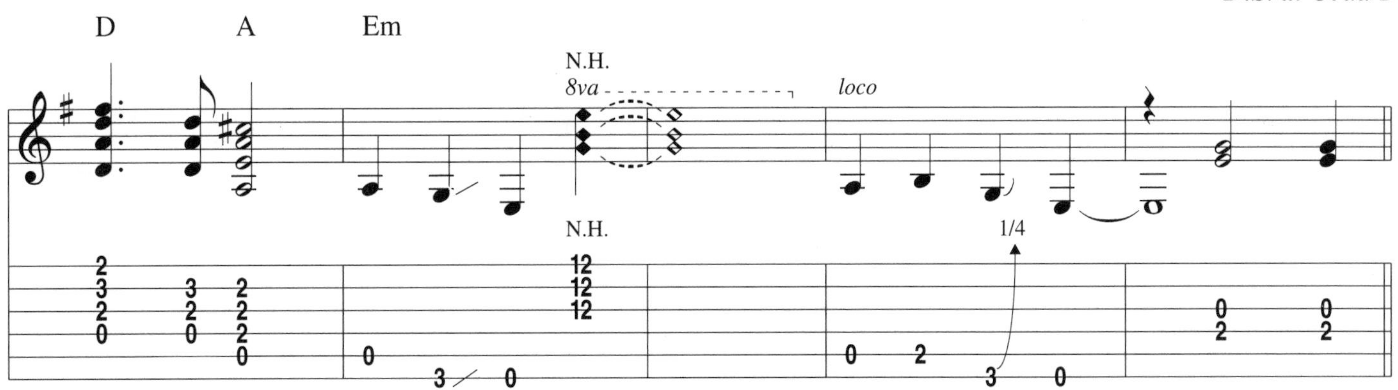

Coda 1

Em

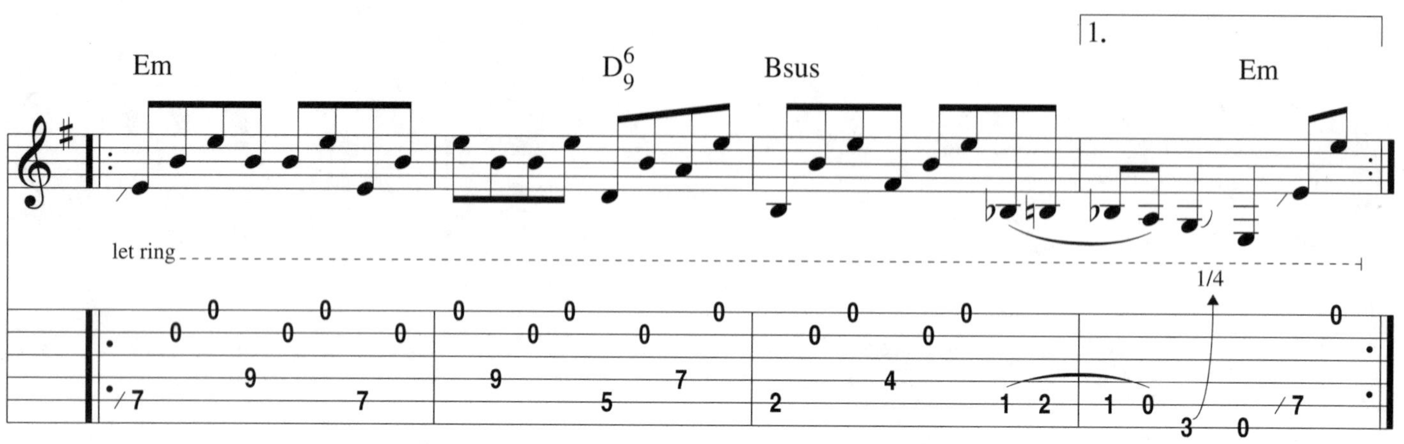
Em
D 6 9
Bsus
1.
Em
let ring
1/4

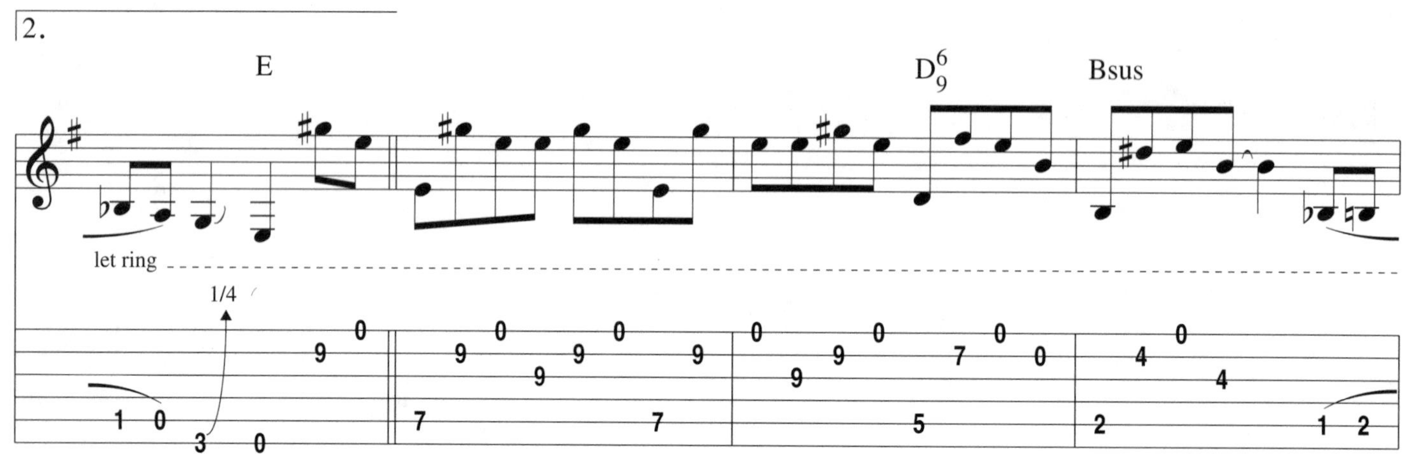
2.
E
D 6 9
Bsus
let ring
1/4

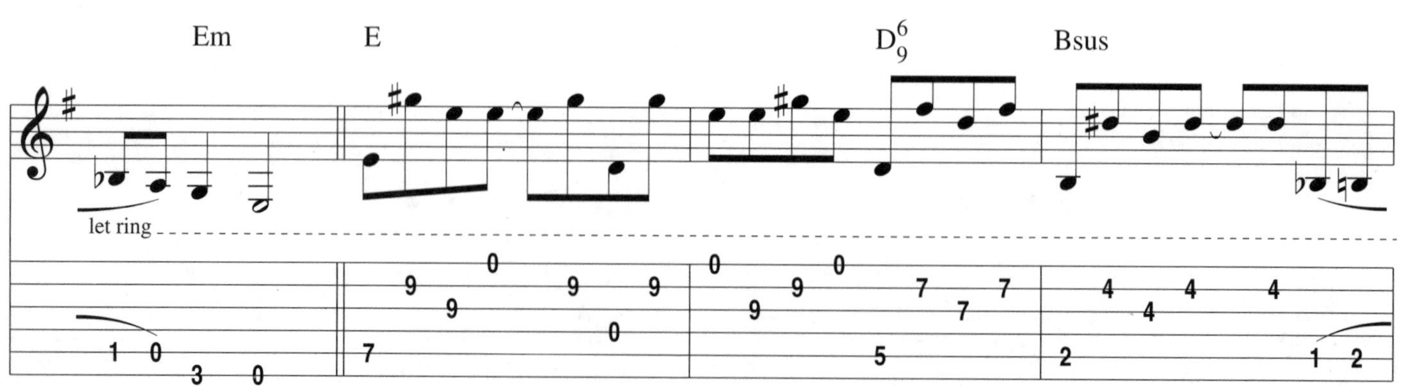
Em
E
D 6 9
Bsus
let ring

♩ = ♩
Bsus
Em
Em
let ring
*R.H. slap and mute strings.

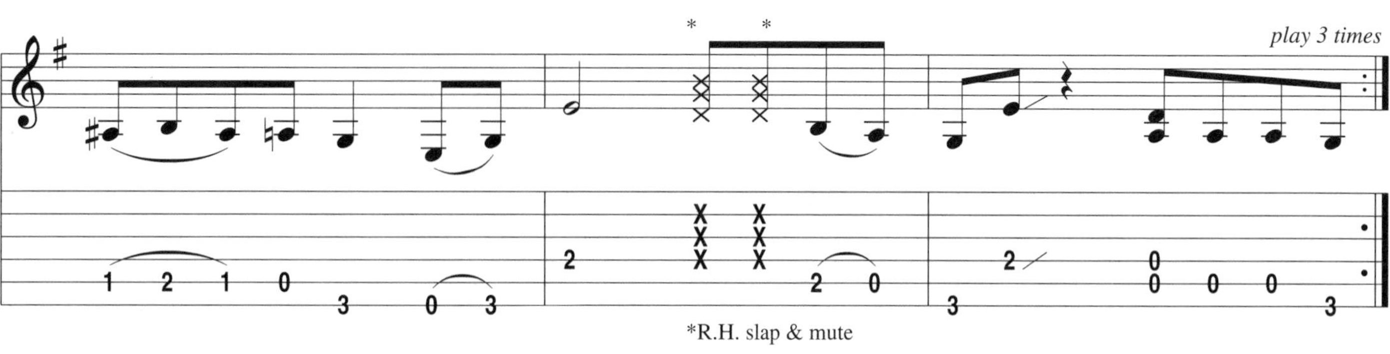

play 3 times
*R.H. slap & mute

Em

D.S.S. al Coda 2
Play 4 times simile

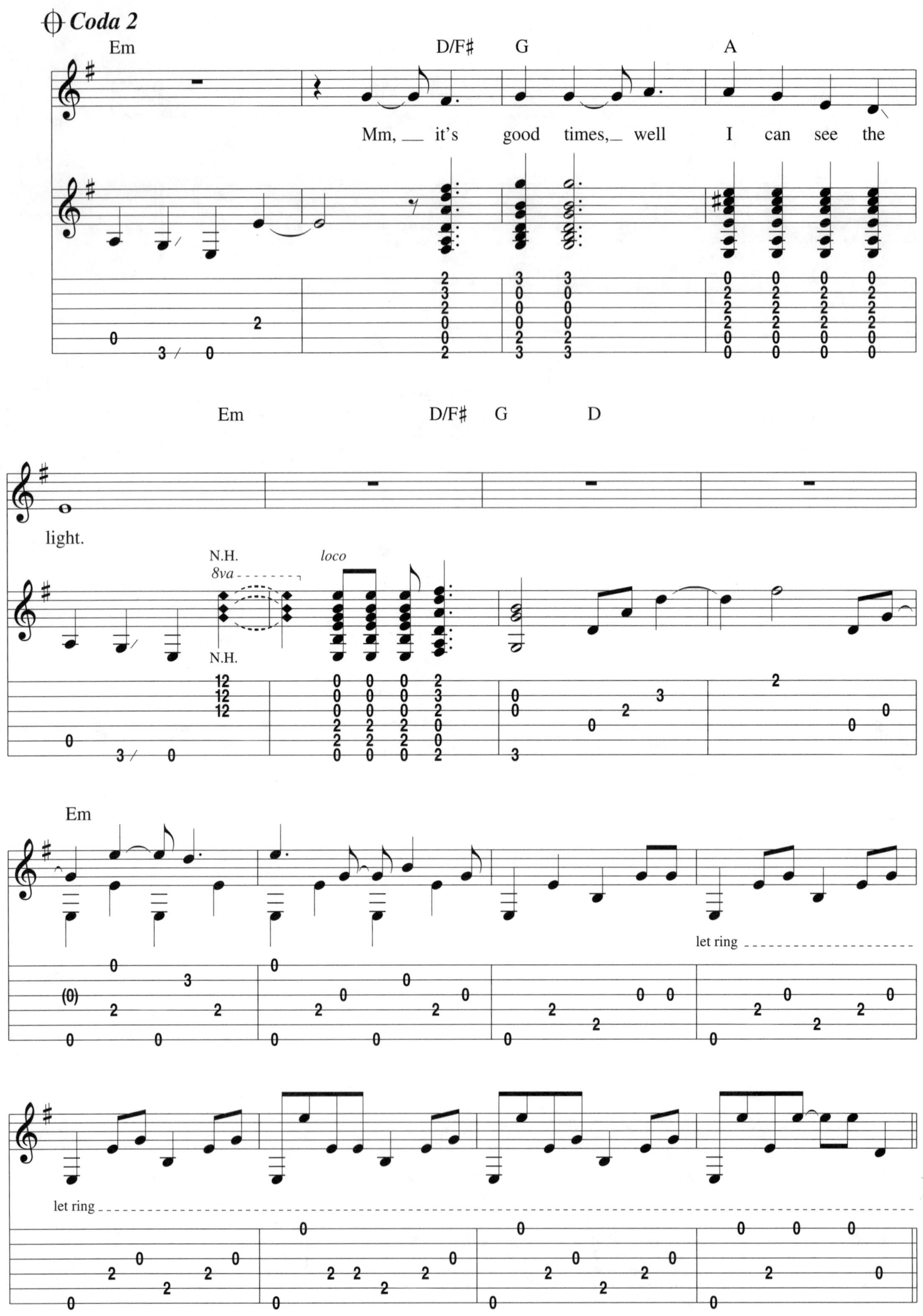
Coda 2
Em
D/F♯
G
A
Mm, it's good times, well I can see the light.
Em
D/F♯
G
D
N.H.
8va
loco
N.H.
Em
let ring
let ring

Em

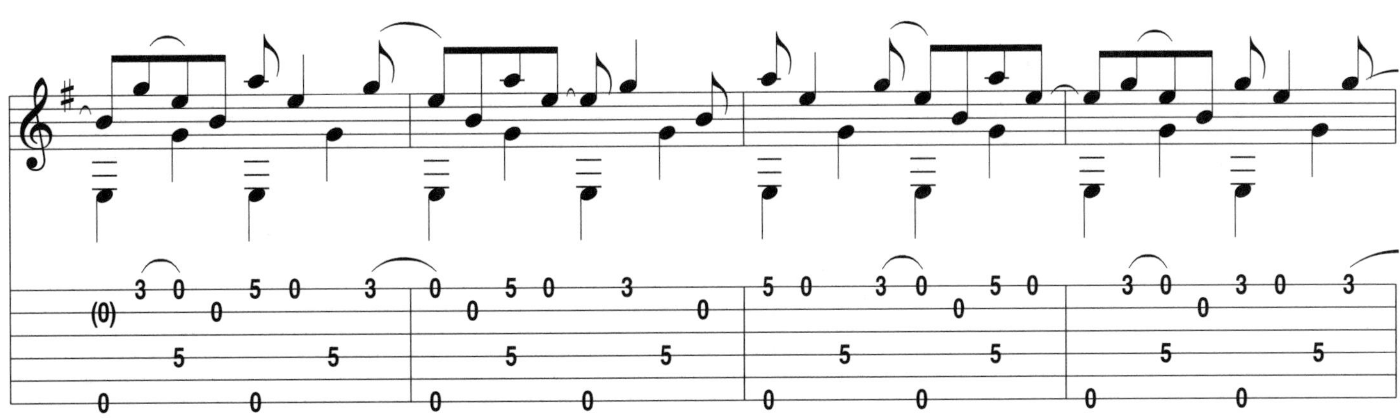
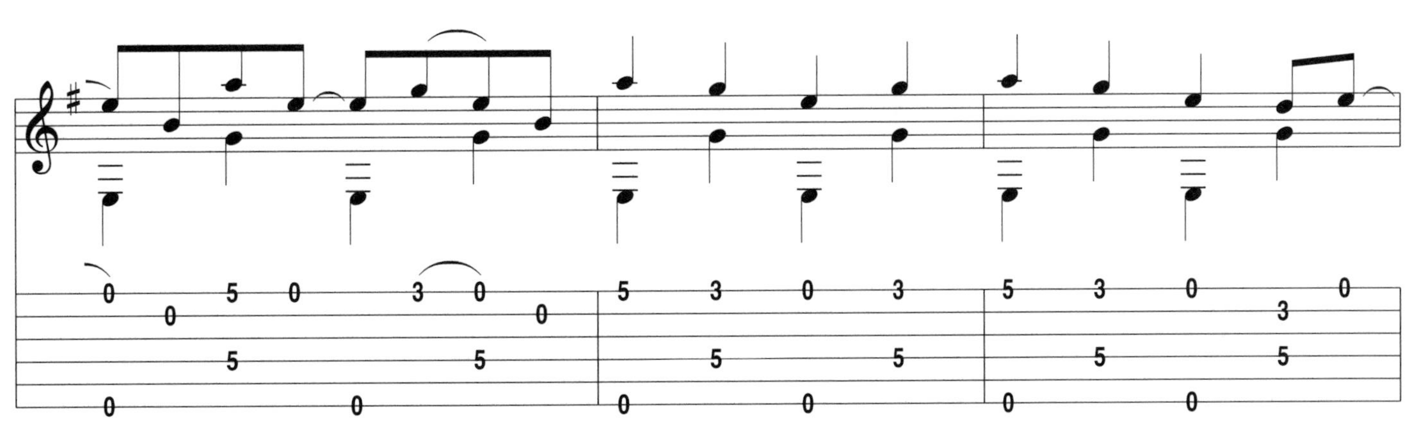

Em7
D7/A

C/G
Fmaj7

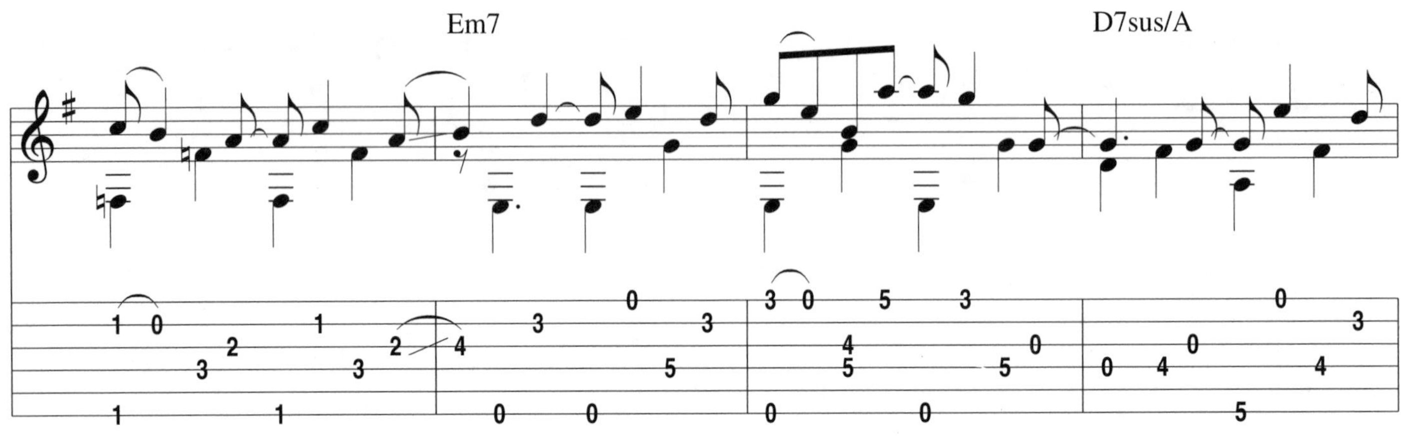
Em7
D7sus/A

C/G
Fmaj7

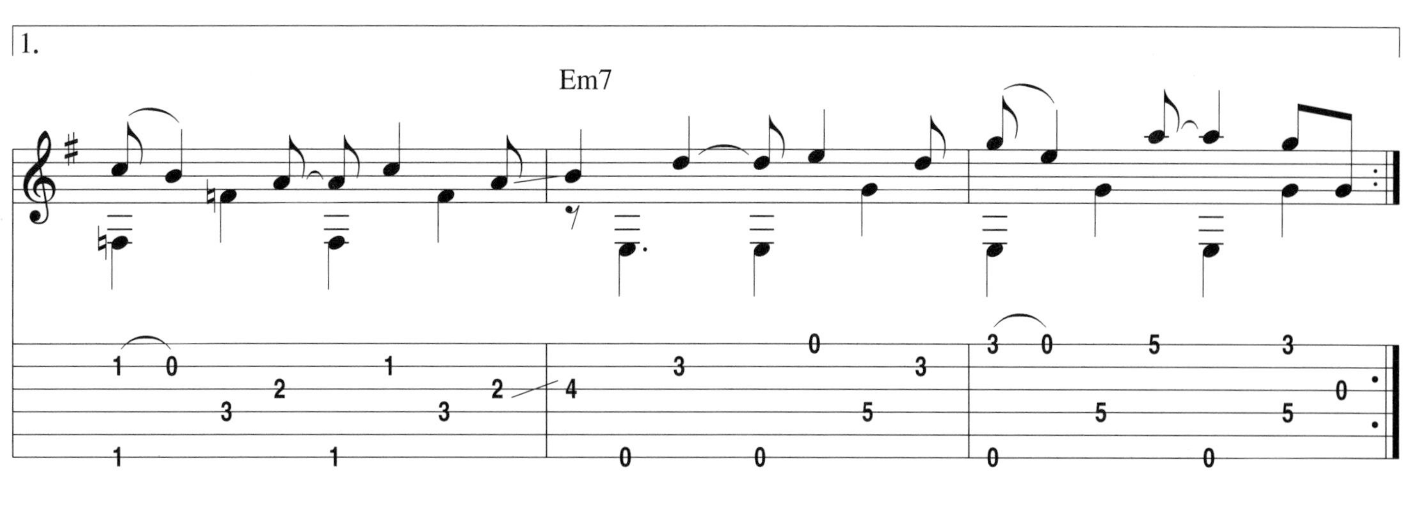
1.
Em7

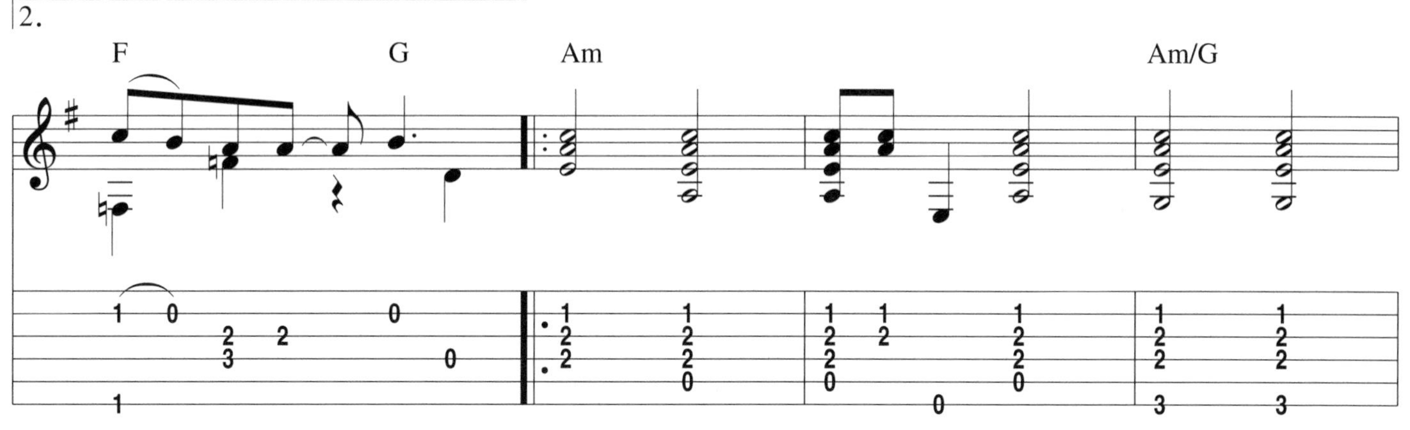
2.
F
G
Am
Am/G

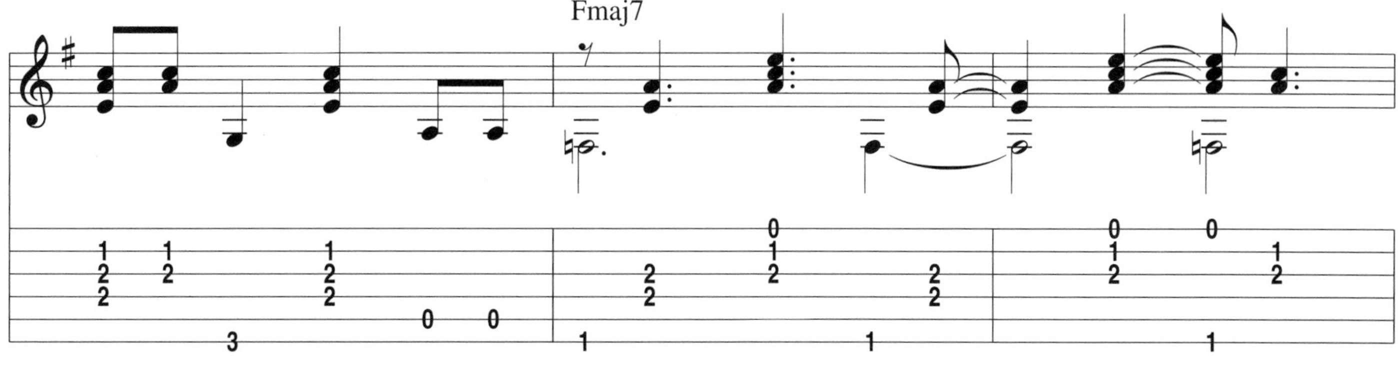
Fmaj7

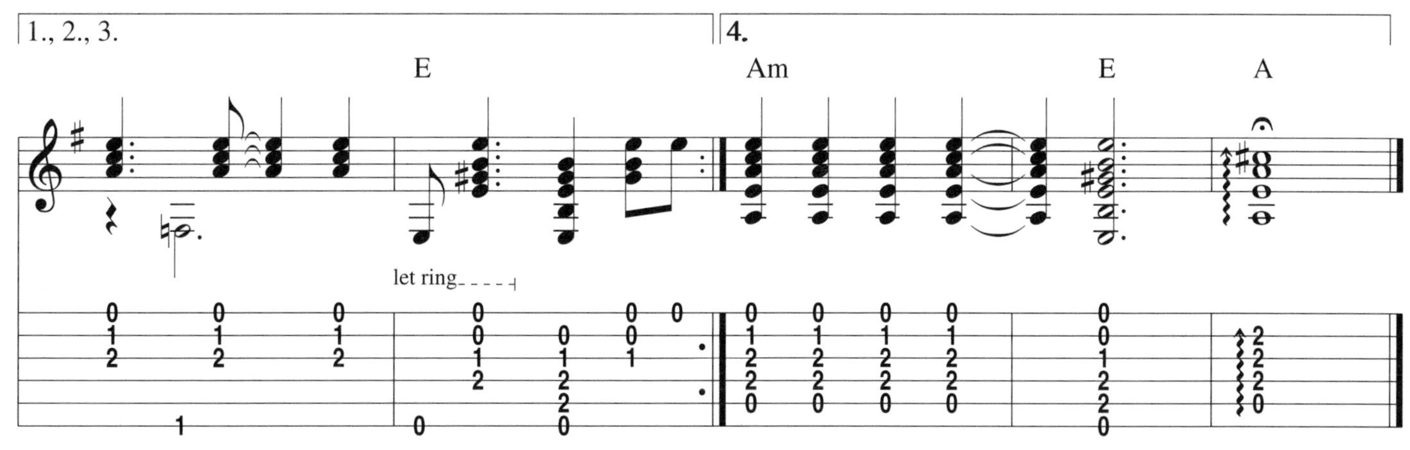
1., 2., 3.
4.
E
Am
E
A
let ring

Additional Lyrics

2. Oh, this road I'm walkin' on,
I see my way.
The paradise I'm livin' for
Each and every day.
Feelin' us together, now pushin' back the night,
Good times, I can see the light.

3. In this sea I'm movin' through,
Feel my life complete.
With the one I'm livin' for
The time is oh, so sweet.
Together now pushin' back the night,
Good times, well, I can see the light.

Been So Long

Words and Music by Jorma Kaukonen

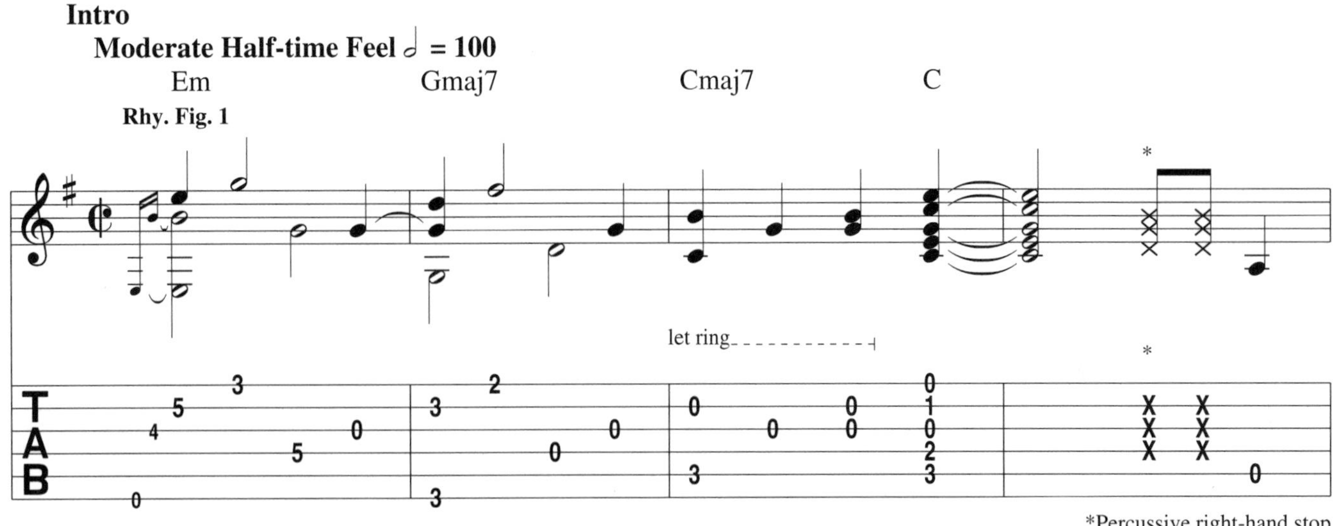

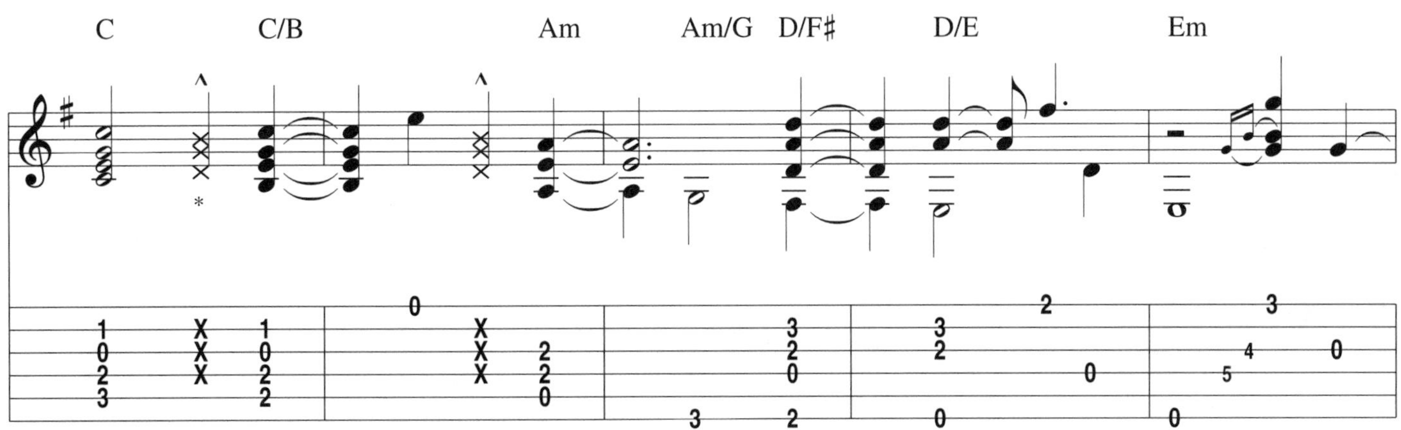

B7
Em
Am

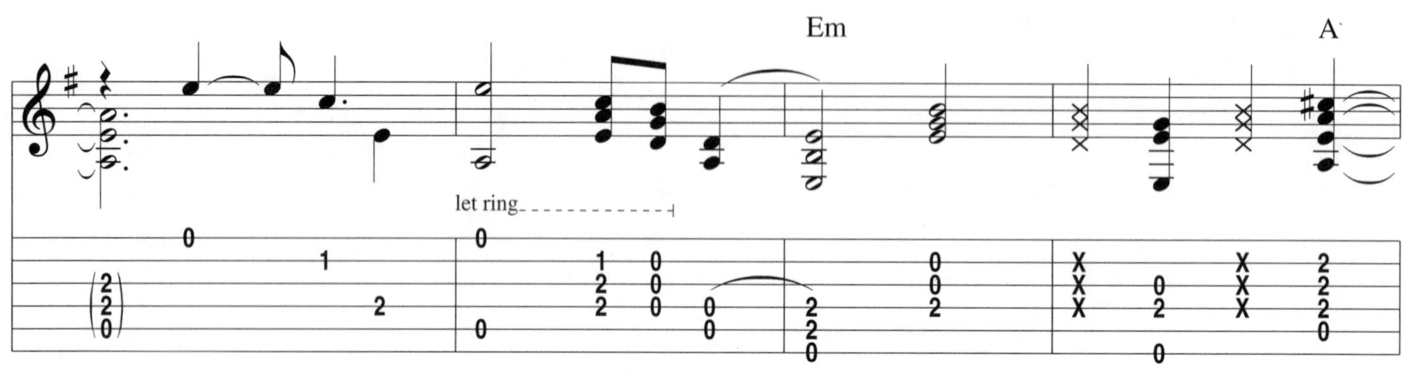
Em
A
let ring

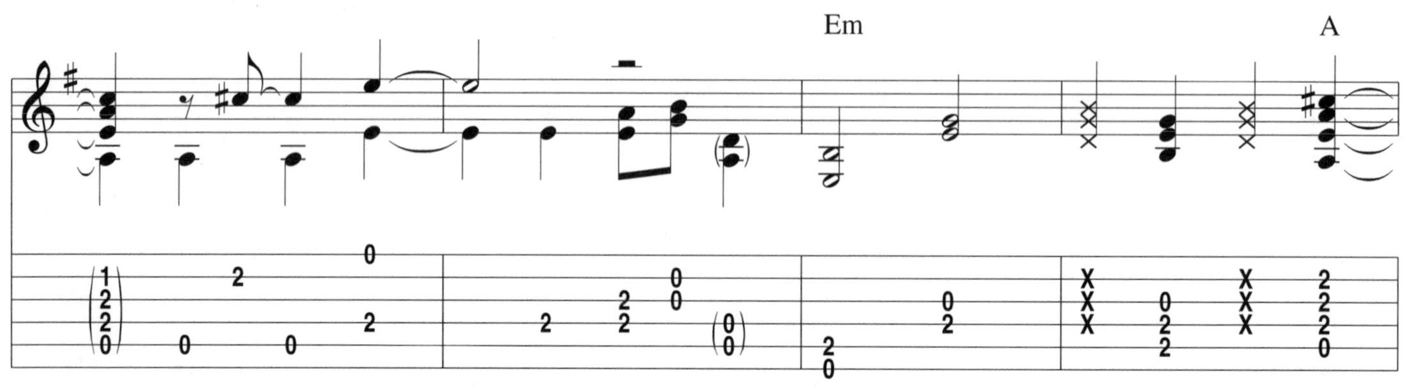
Em
A

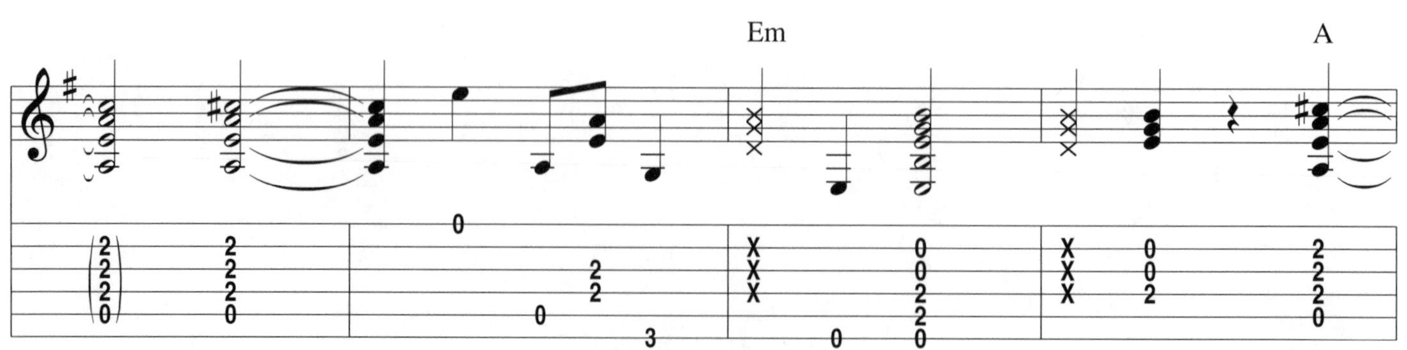
Em
A

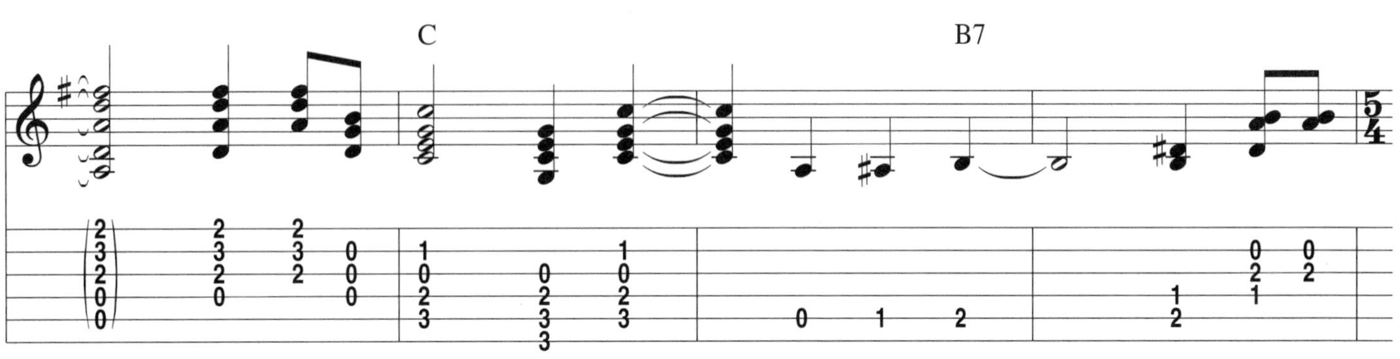

*Implied harmony

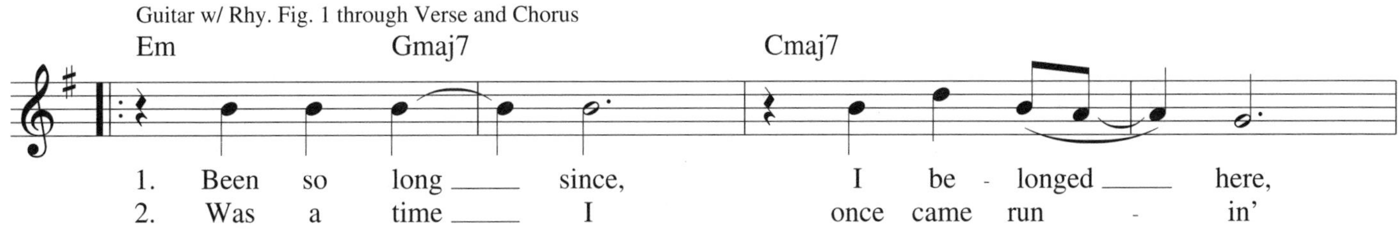

C6 C/B Am Am/G D/F♯ D/E
ev - er since ___ I ___ lost ___ my way, ___ yeah.
down the street ___ we ___ used ___ to live ___

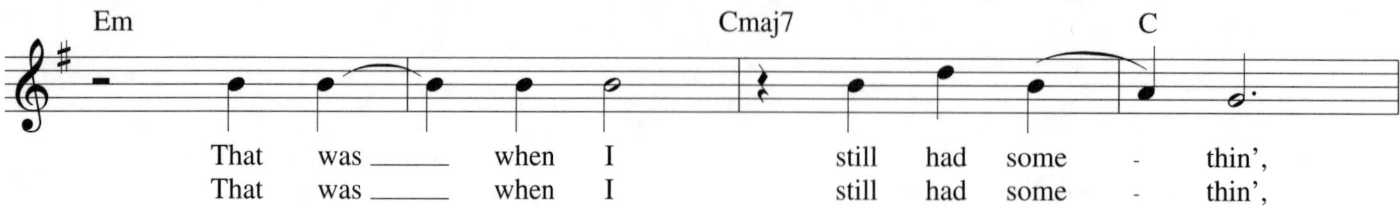
Em Cmaj7 C
That was ___ when I still had some - thin',
That was ___ when I still had some - thin',

B7 Chorus Em
spe - cial left for me to say ___ un - to you. ___
spe - cial left for me to give ___ well,

A Em A
Just to see your _ smile ___

Em A
Laugh and look at ___ me, ___

Em
A
1. when I held you close
2. I held you tight
in the morn - in', child,

Em
D
C
well, it's been so long since I've felt at home

C
B7
B7/F♯
B7
B7/A
C7/G
B7/F♯
in the mir - ror.

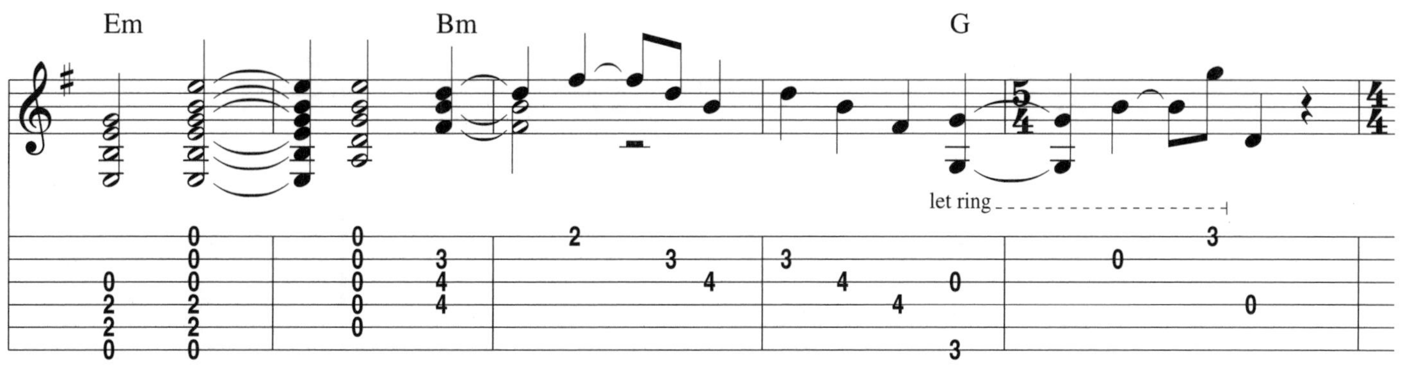
Em
Bm
G
let ring

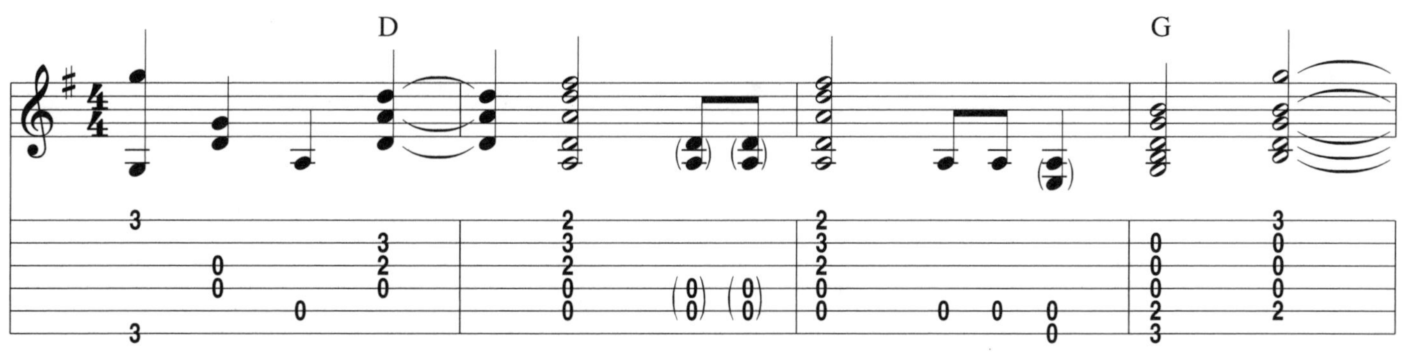
D
G

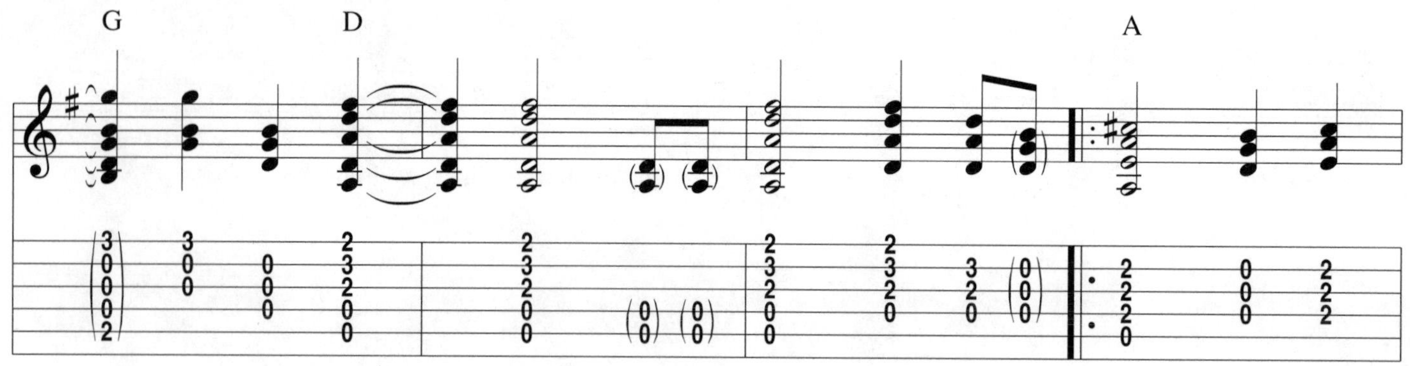
G
D
A

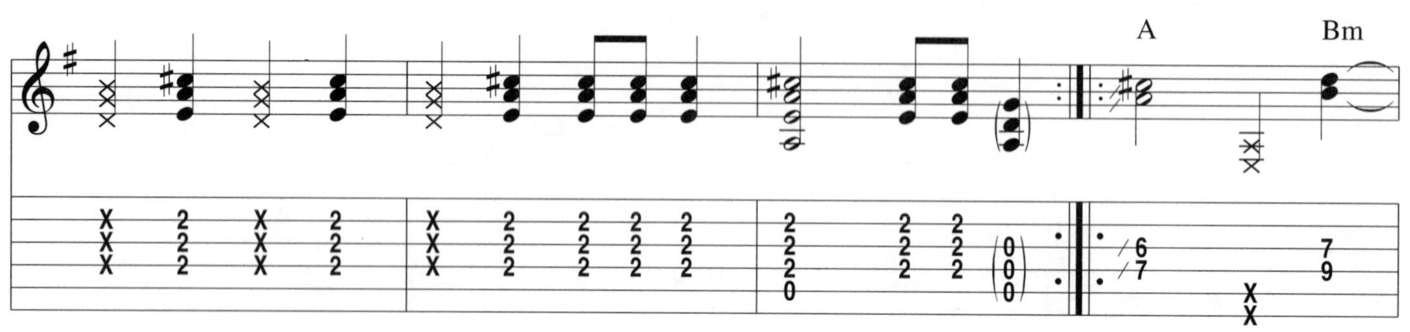
A
Bm

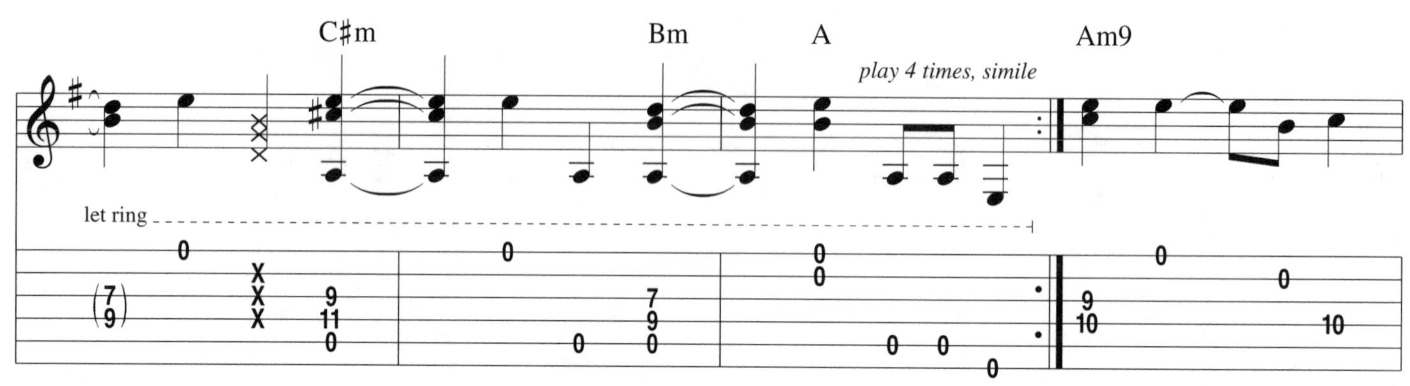
C♯m
Bm
A
play 4 times, simile
Am9
let ring

B♭ ♭5 ♭9 / A
Aadd9
A9no3rd

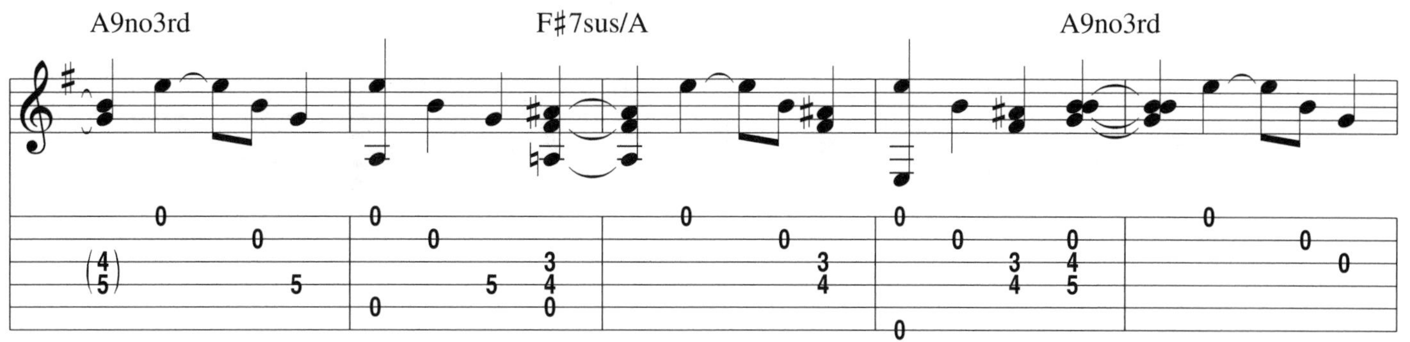
A9no3rd
F♯7sus/A
A9no3rd

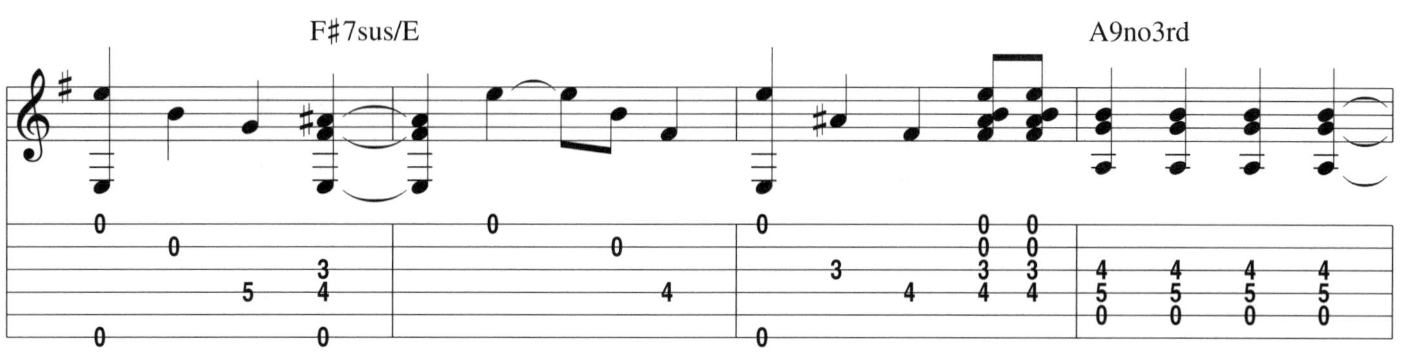
F♯7sus/E
A9no3rd

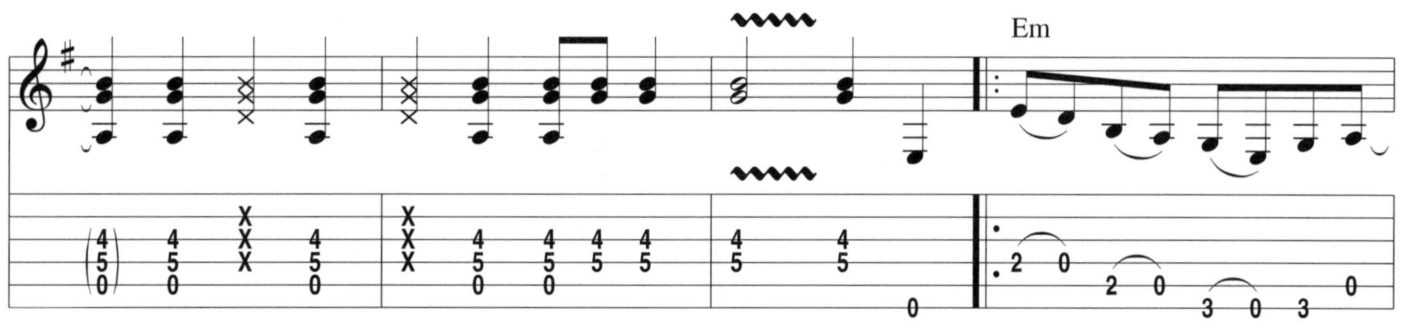
Em

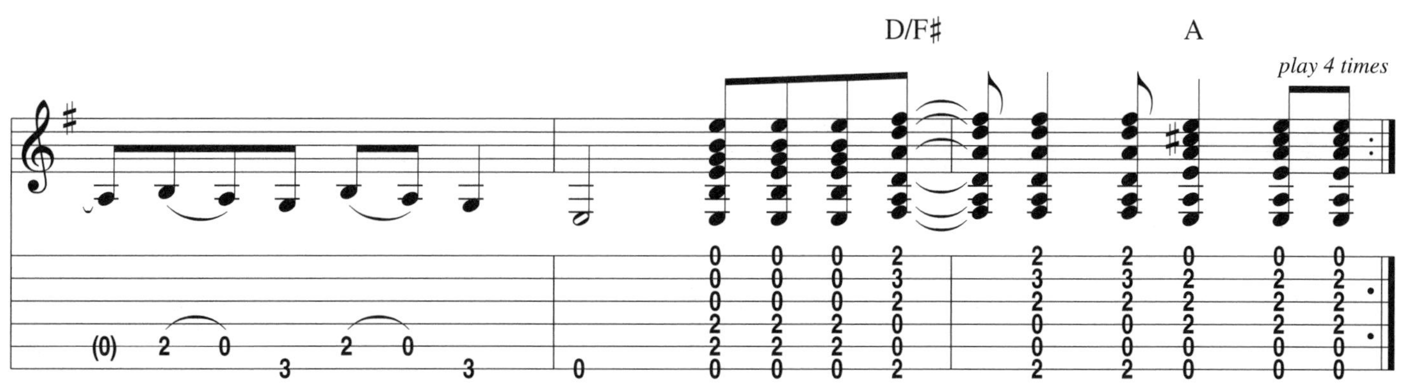
D/F♯
A
play 4 times

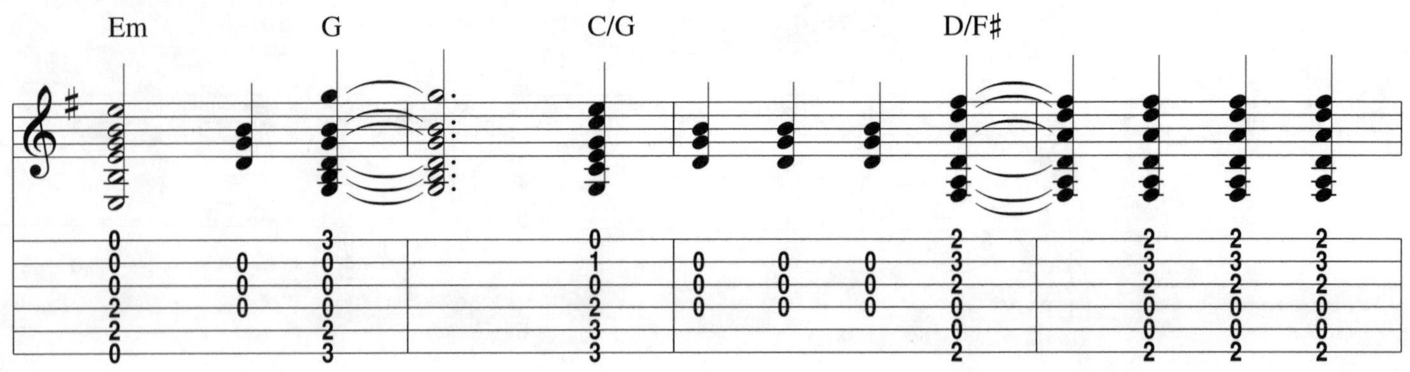
Em
G
C/G
D/F♯

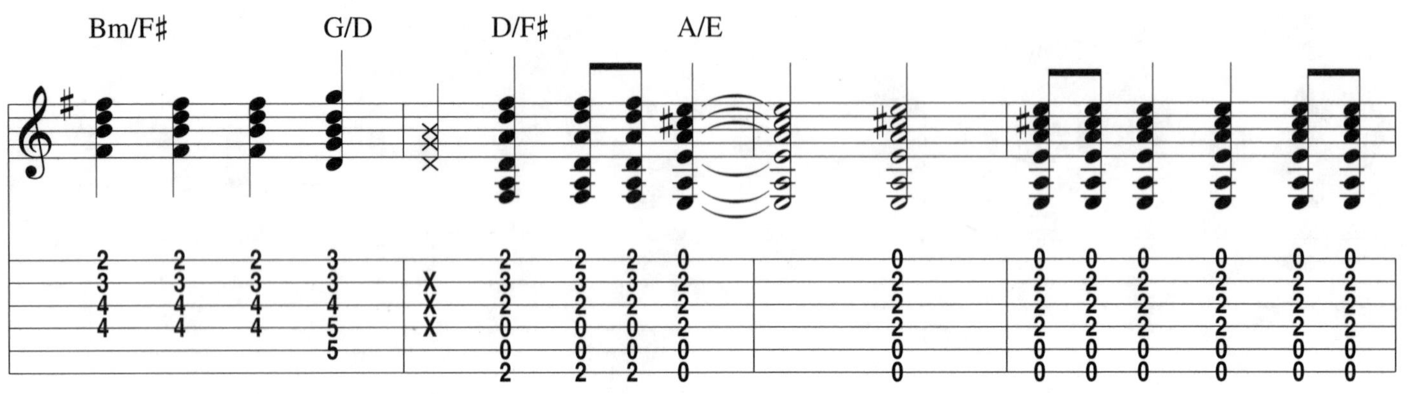
Bm/F♯
G/D
D/F♯
A/E

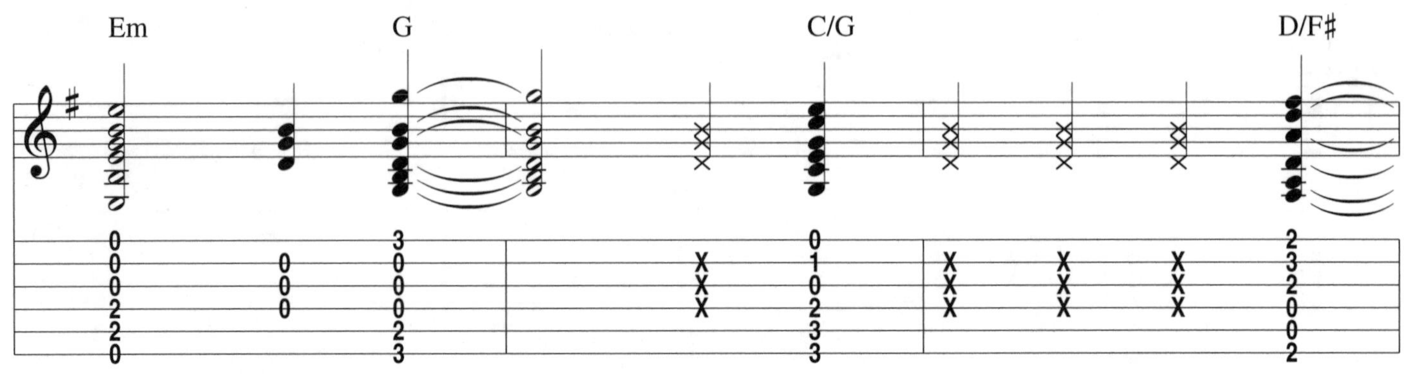
Em
G
C/G
D/F♯

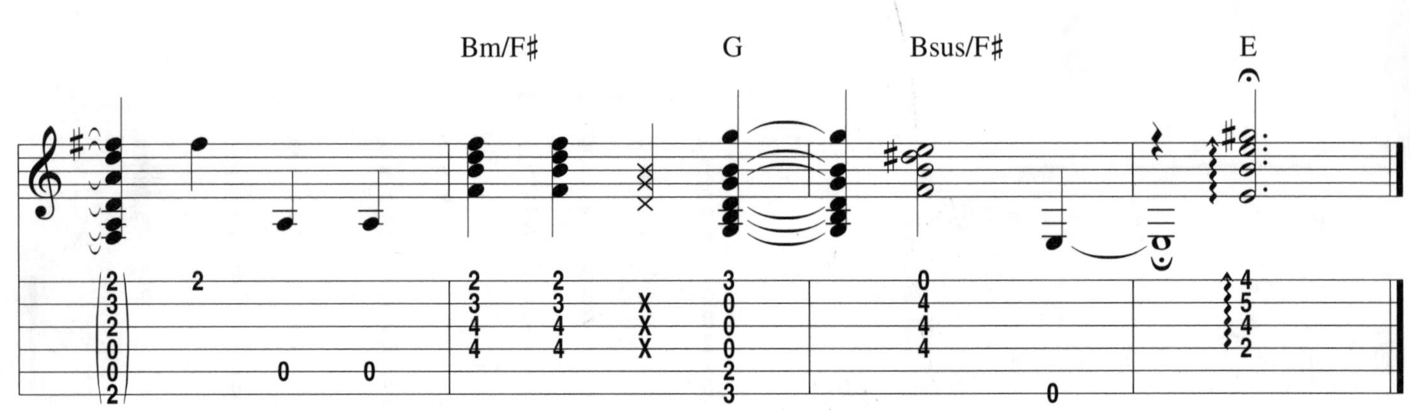
Bm/F♯
G
Bsus/F♯
E

38 Mann's Fate

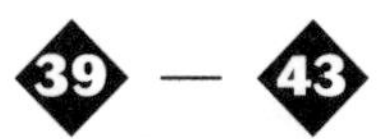

Words and Music by Jorma Kaukonen

A

Moderate Half-time Feel 𝅗𝅥 = 104

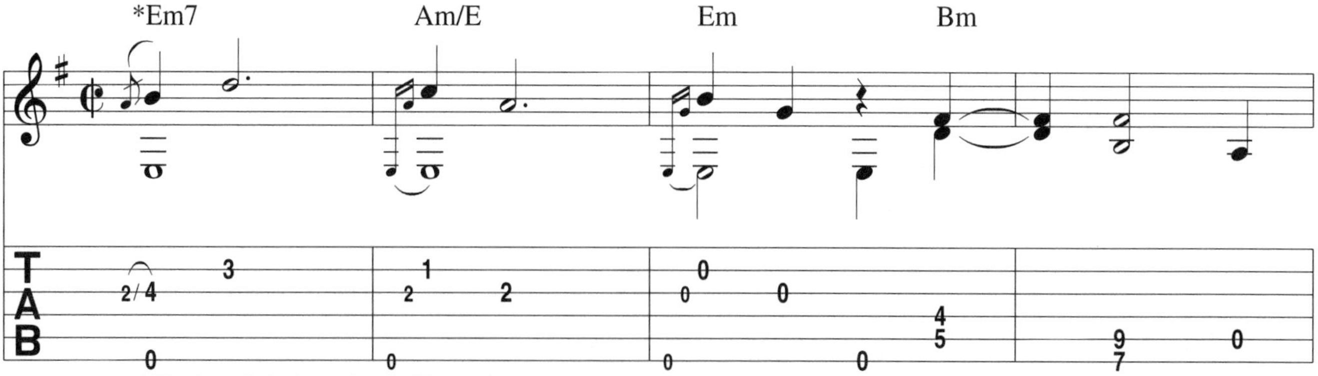

*Em7 Am/E Em Bm

*Chord symbols denote implied harmony

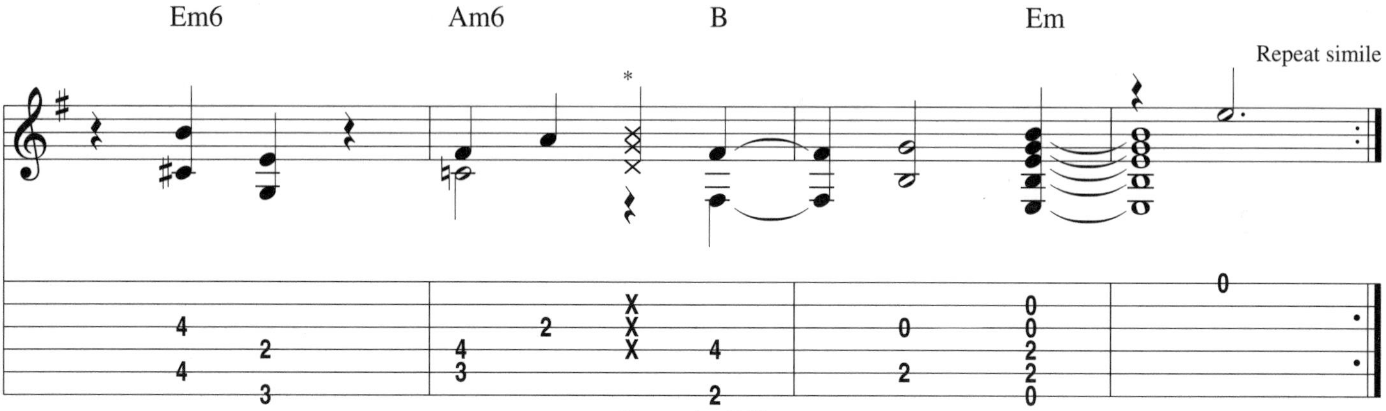

Em6 Am6 B Em

Repeat simile

*Percussive R.H. stop

B

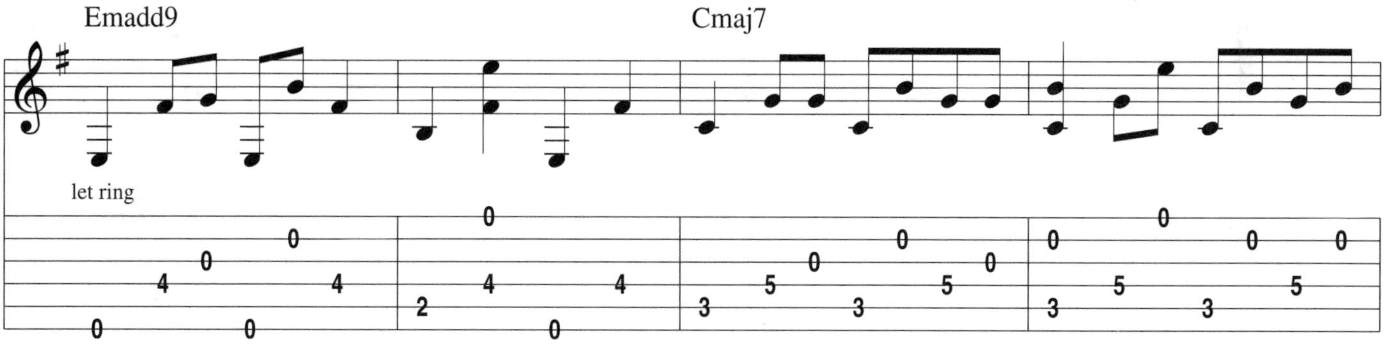

Emadd9 Cmaj7

let ring

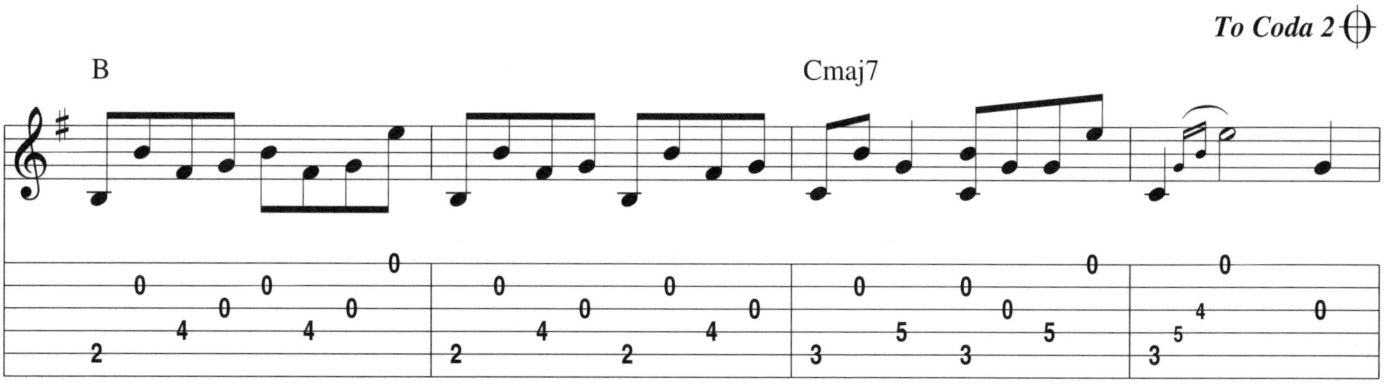

B Cmaj7

To Coda 2 ⊕

Cmaj7♯11
Cmaj7

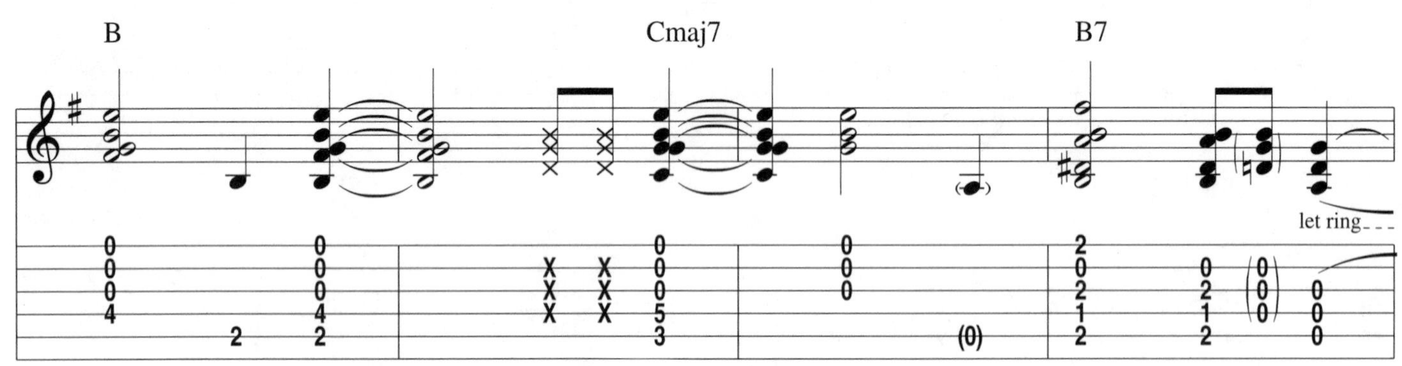
B
Cmaj7
B7
let ring

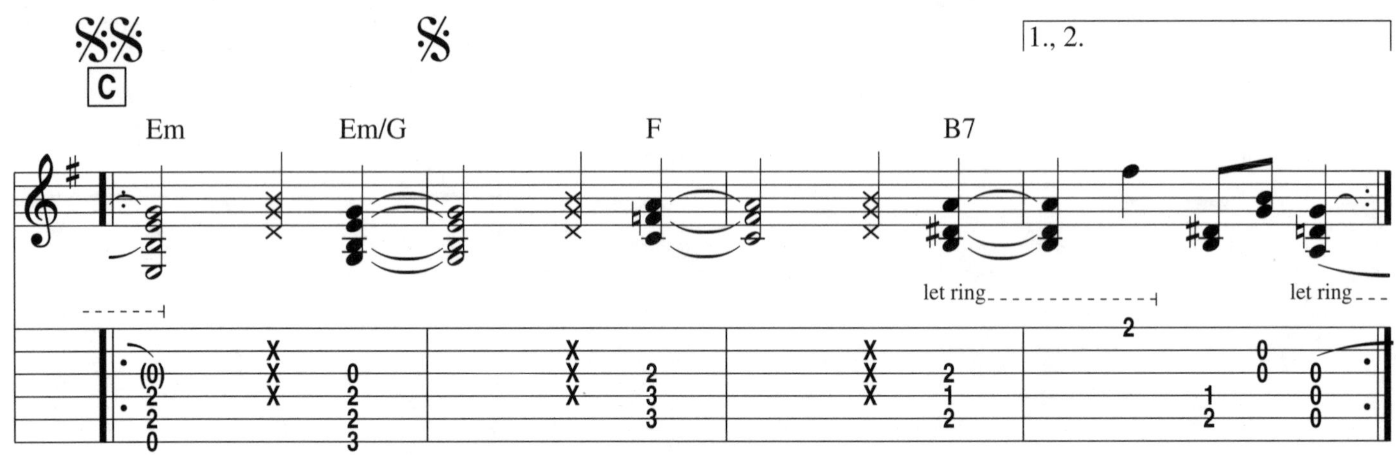
C
1., 2.
Em
Em/G
F
B7
let ring
let ring

3.
Em

3rd time **To Coda 3** 𝄌

2nd time **To Coda 1** 𝄌

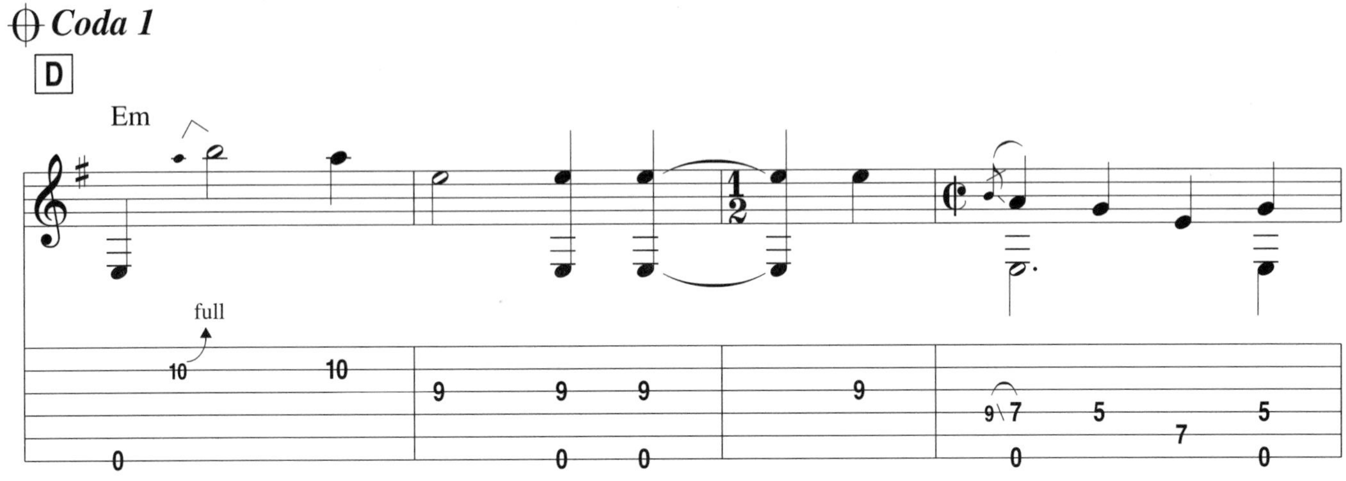

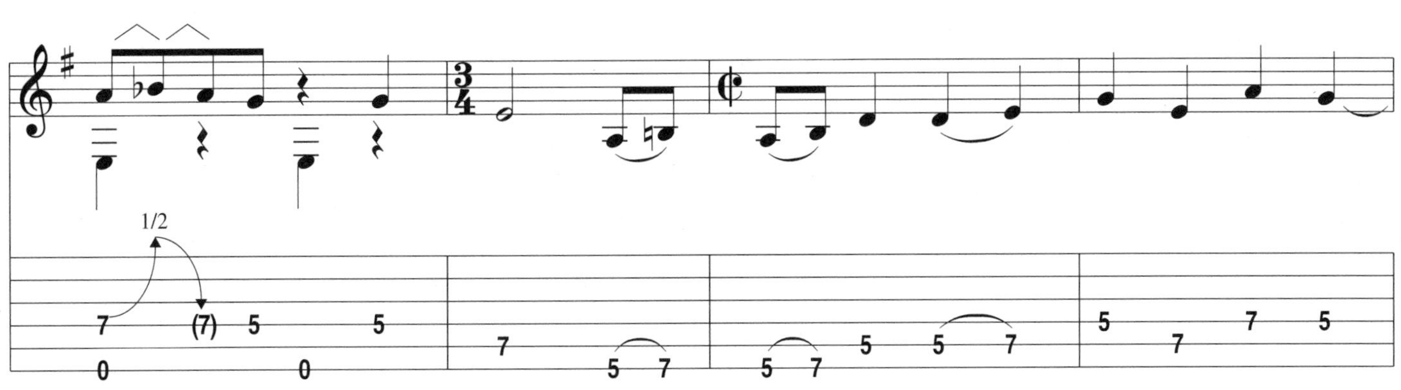

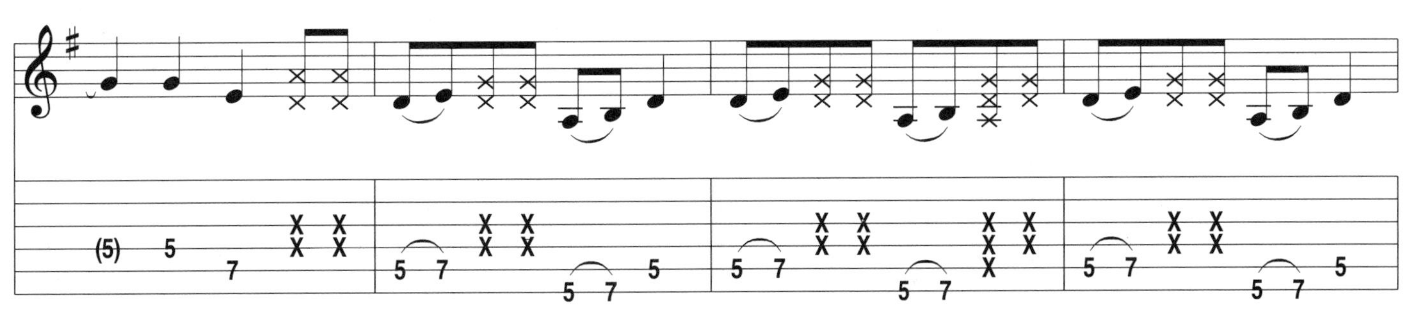

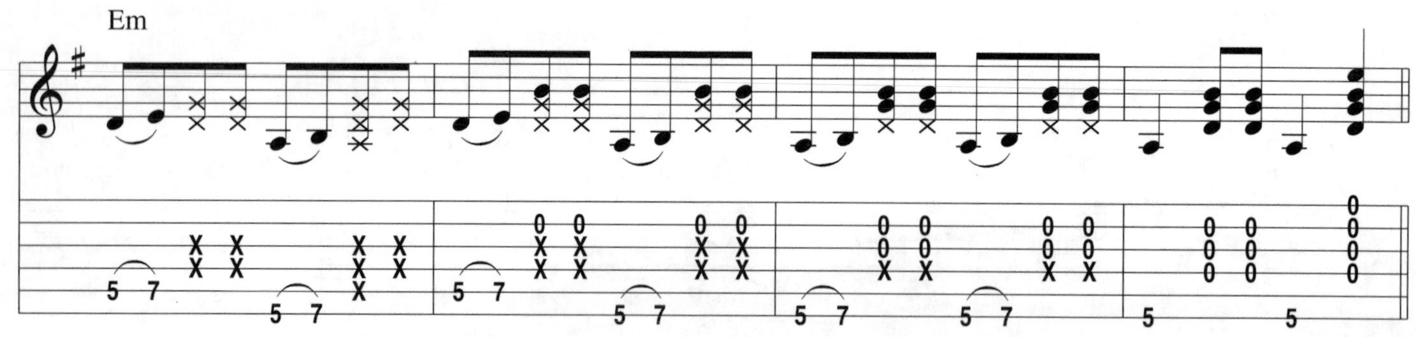
Em

E
D.C. al Coda 2
Em7
B
play 4 times
let ring

Coda 2

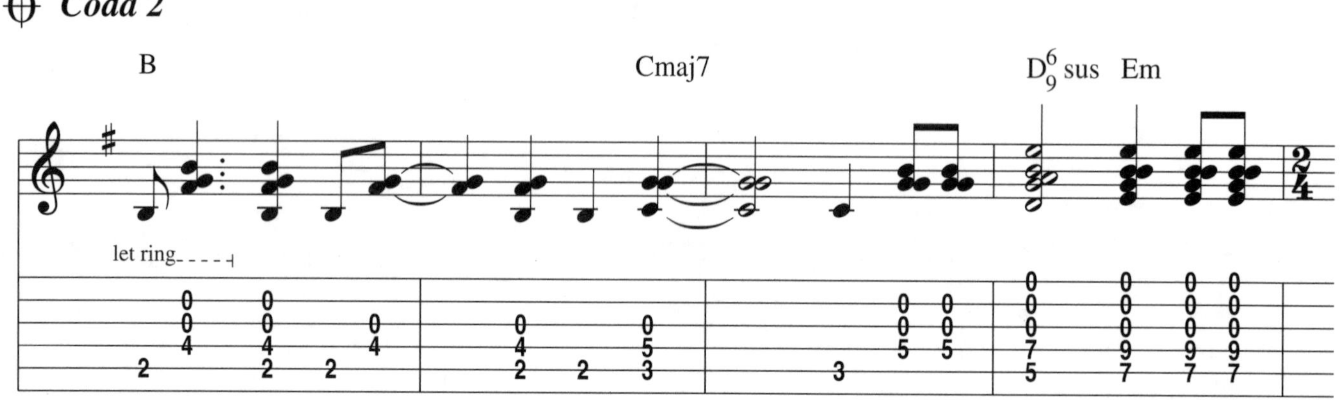
B
Cmaj7
D^6_9 sus
Em
let ring

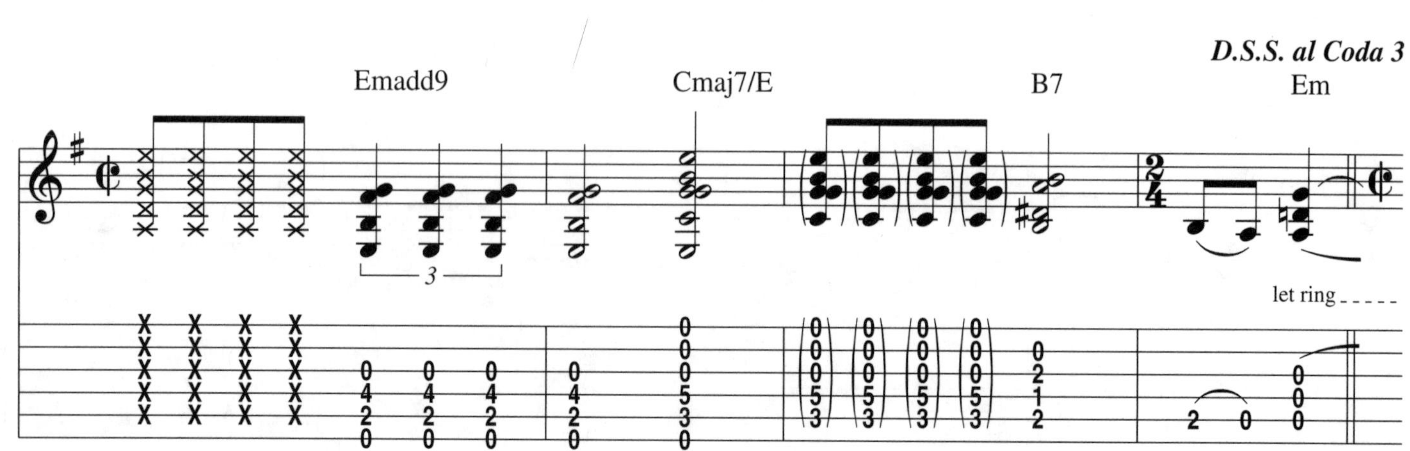
D.S.S. al Coda 3
Emadd9
Cmaj7/E
B7
Em
let ring

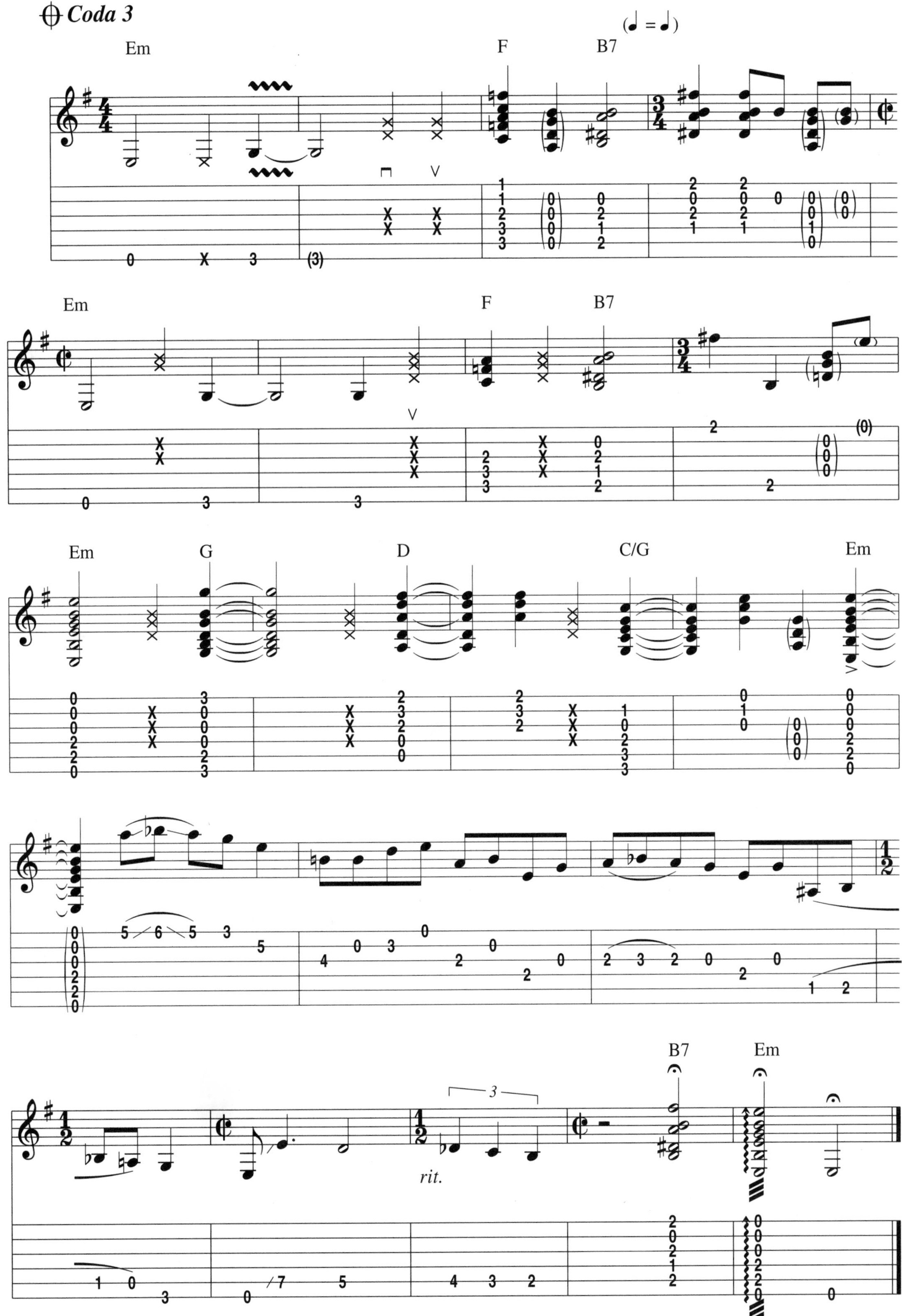
Coda 3
Em
F
B7
Em
F
B7
Em
G
D
C/G
Em
rit.
B7
Em

45 Genesis

Words and Music by Jorma Kaukonen

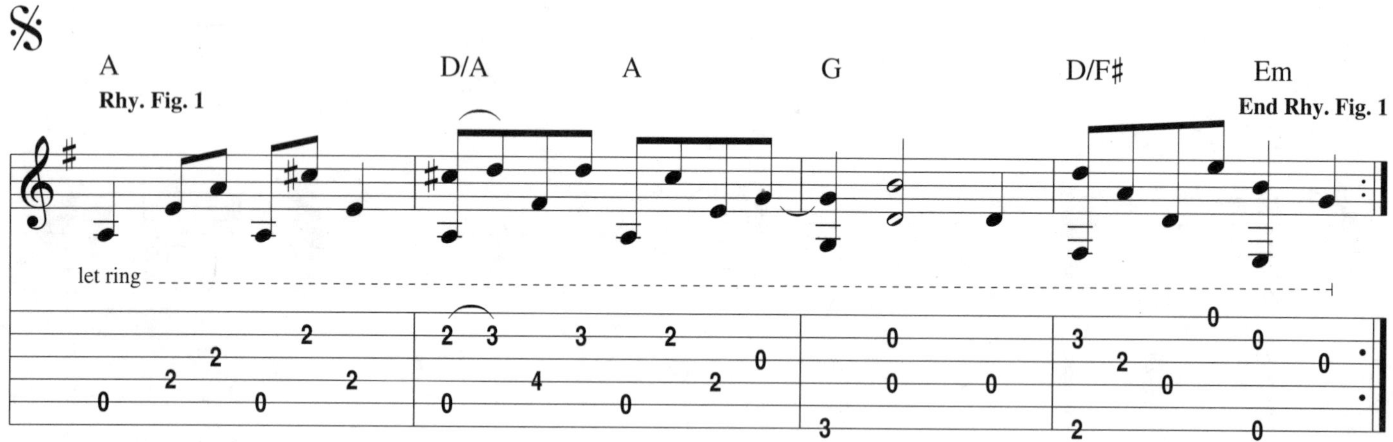

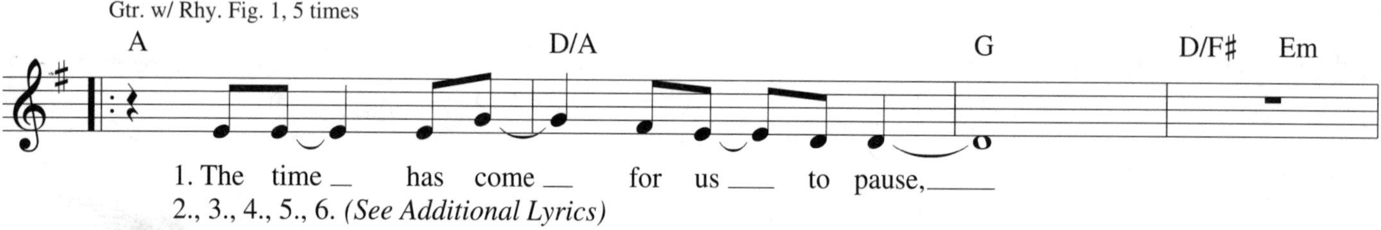

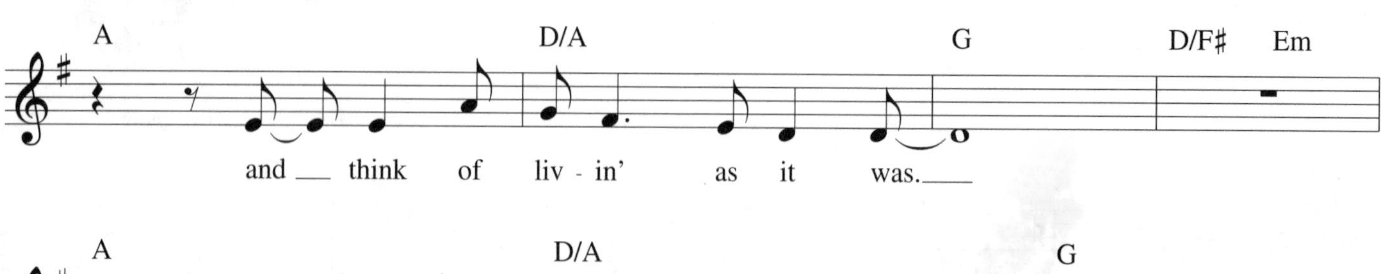

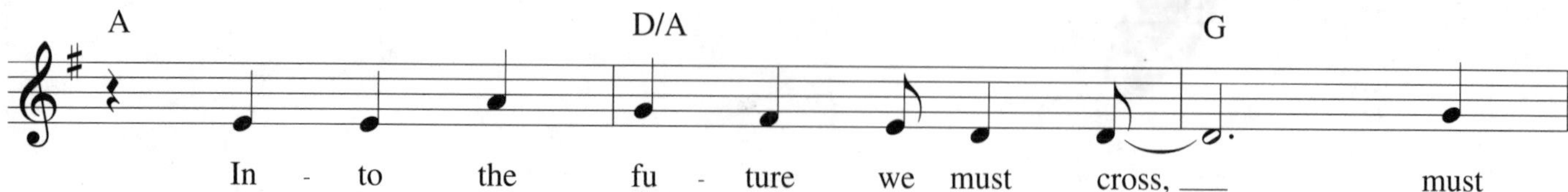

D/F♯
Em
A
D/A
G
cross.
Yeah, I'd like to go with you.

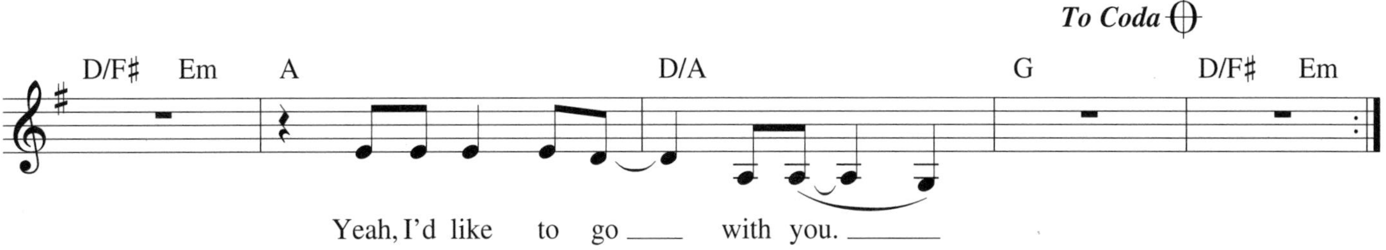
To Coda
D/F♯
Em
A
D/A
G
D/F♯
Em
Yeah, I'd like to go with you.

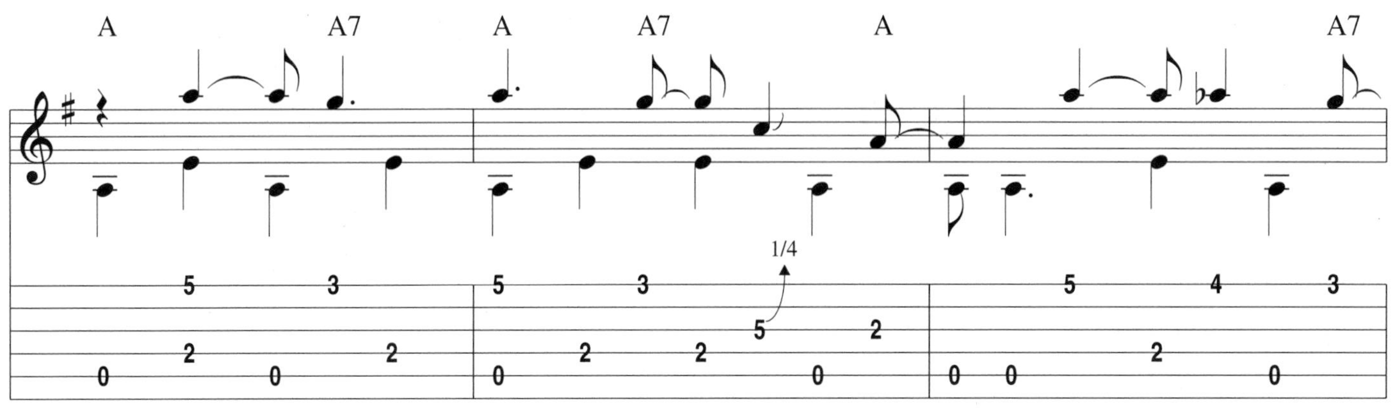
A
A7
A
A7
A
A7
1/4

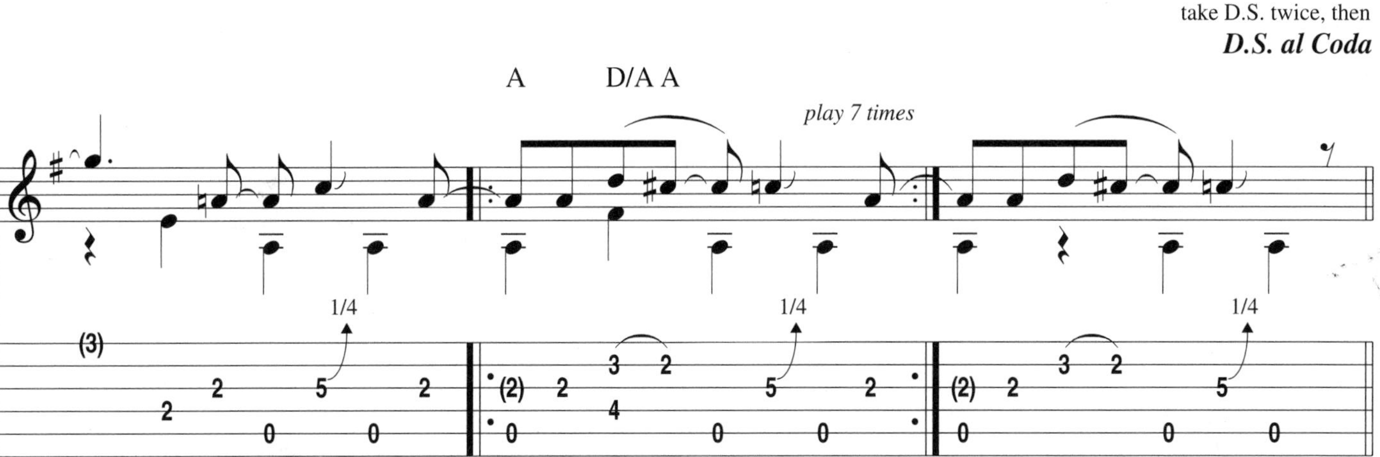
take D.S. twice, then
D.S. al Coda
A
D/A A
play 7 times
1/4

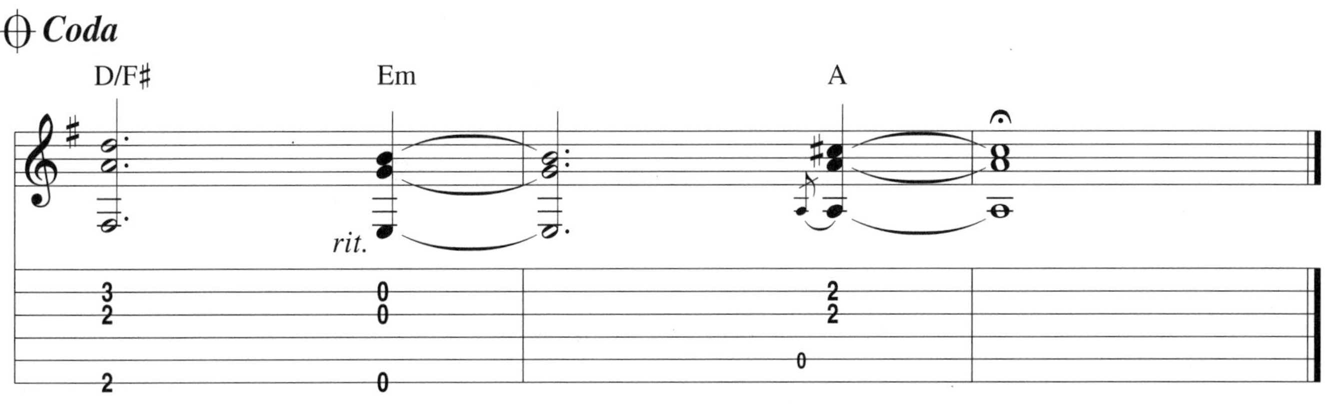
Coda
D/F♯
Em
A
rit.

Additional Lyrics

2. You say I'm harder than a wall,
A marble shaft about to fall.
I love you dearer than them all, them all.
And I'd like to stay with you,
Yeah, I'd like to stay with you.

3. Well, as we walked into the day,
Skies of blue have turned to gray.
I might have not been fair to say, to say,
"I never looked away,
I never looked away."

4. And though I'm feelin' you inside,
My life is rollin' with the tide.
I'd like to see it be an open ride.
Goin' along with you,
And I go along with you.

5. The time we borrowed from ourselves
Can't stay within a vaulted well.
The river turned into a wind.
I like to be with you.
Well, I'd like to be with you.

6. And then we came out into view,
And there I found myself with you,
When we then felt like somethin' new, 'thin' new.
Goin' along with you.
And I go along with you.

48 Watersong

49 — 53

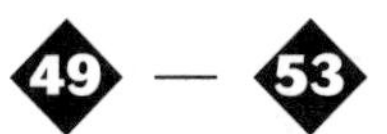

Words and Music by Jorma Kaukonen

Open G Tuning

(1) = D (4) = D

(2) = B (5) = G

(3) = G (6) = D

A

Moderate Half-time Feel 𝅗𝅥 = 94

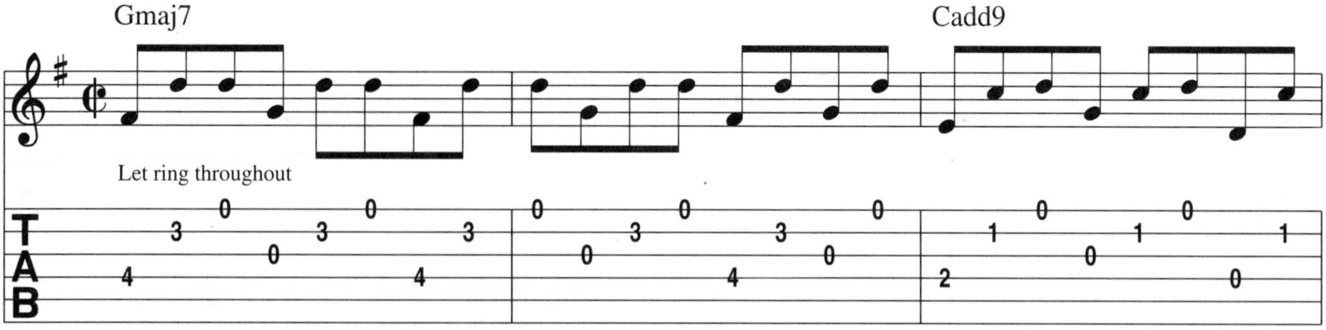

Gmaj7
Cadd9
Let ring throughout

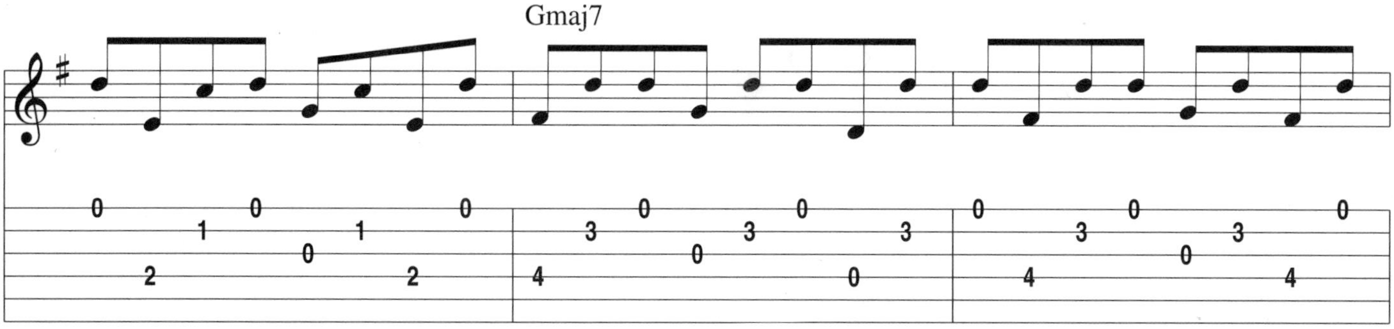

Gmaj7

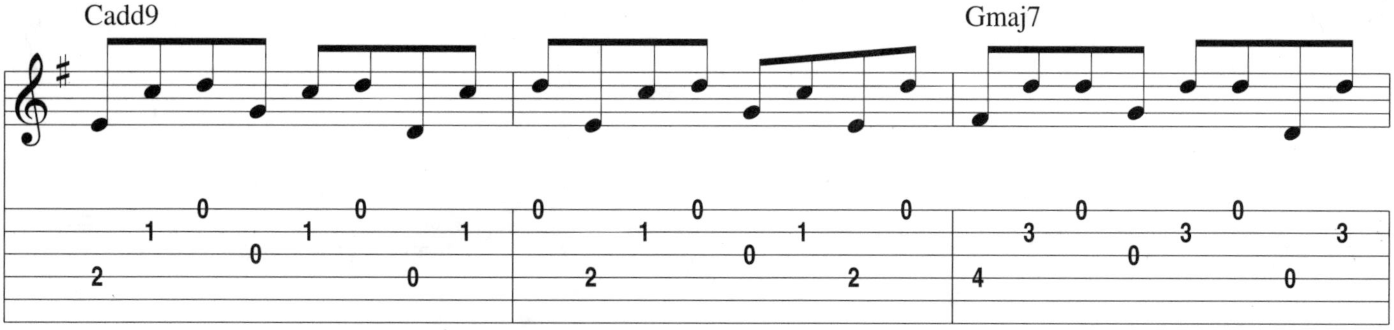

Cadd9
Gmaj7

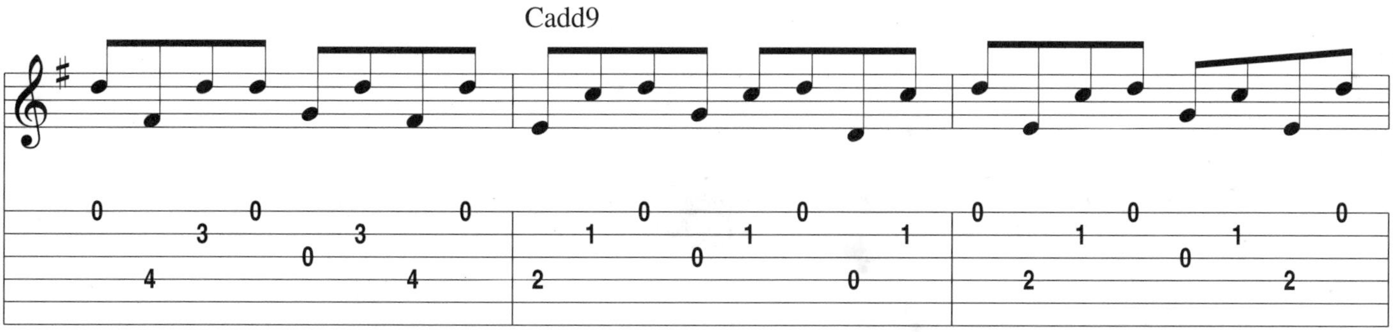

Cadd9

Gmaj7
Cadd9

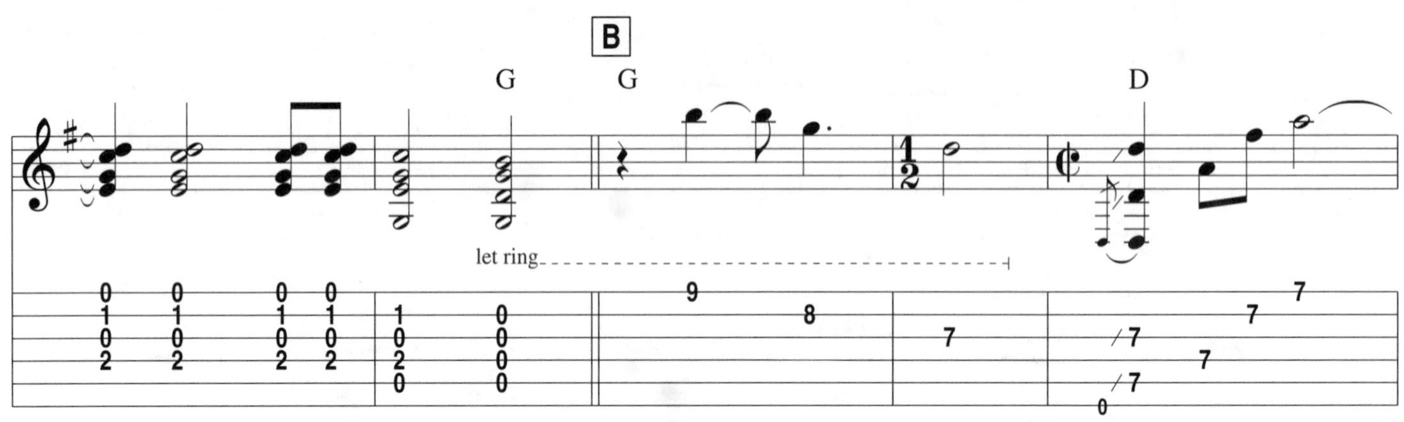
B
G
G
D
let ring

G9no3rd
C

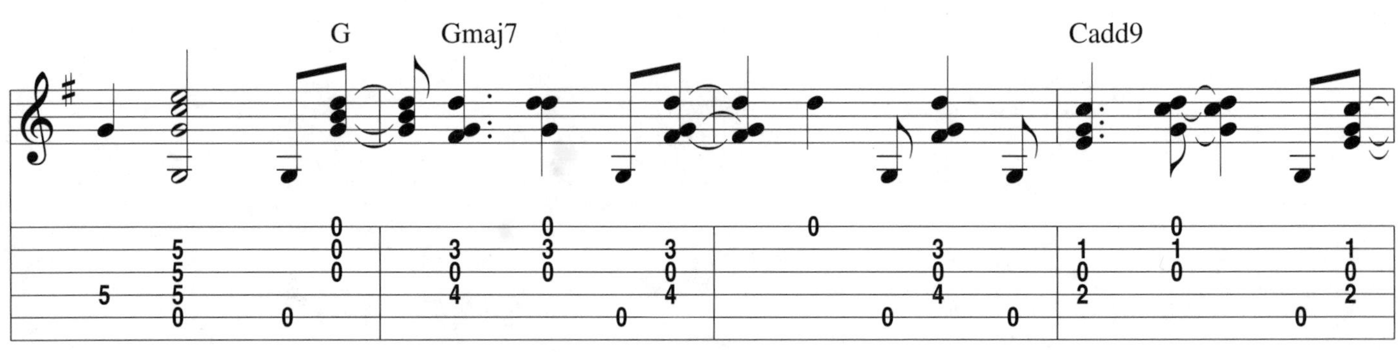
G
Gmaj7
Cadd9

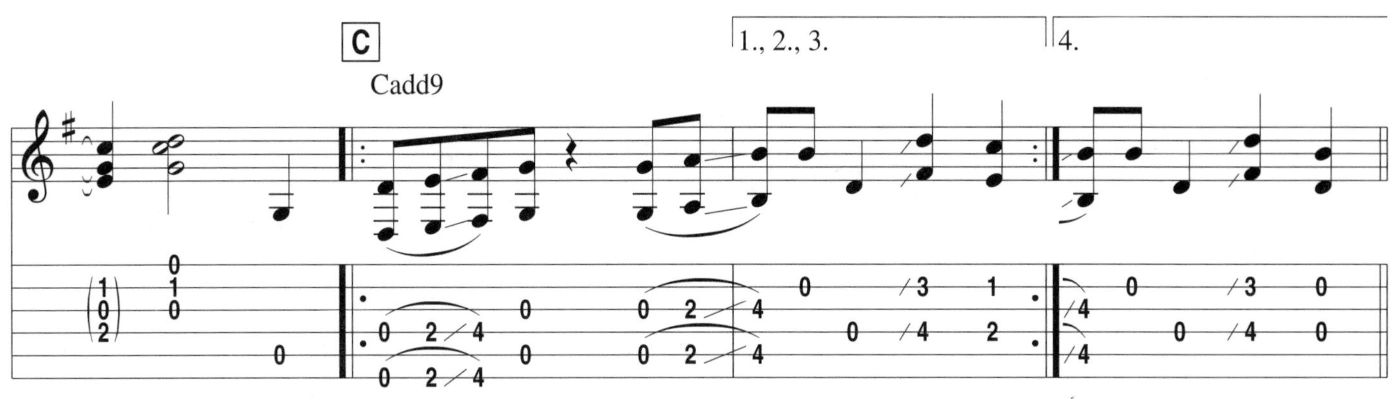
C
Cadd9
1., 2., 3.
4.

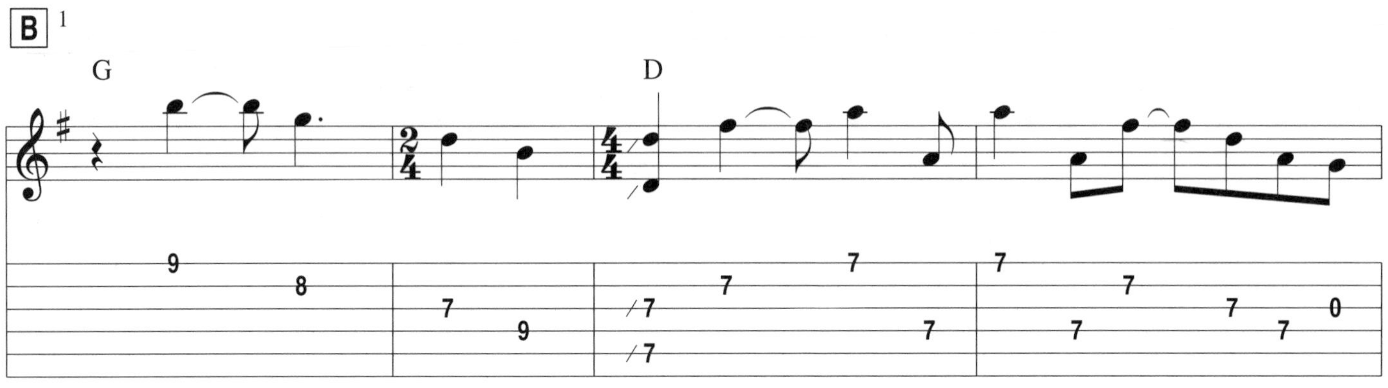
B
1
G
D

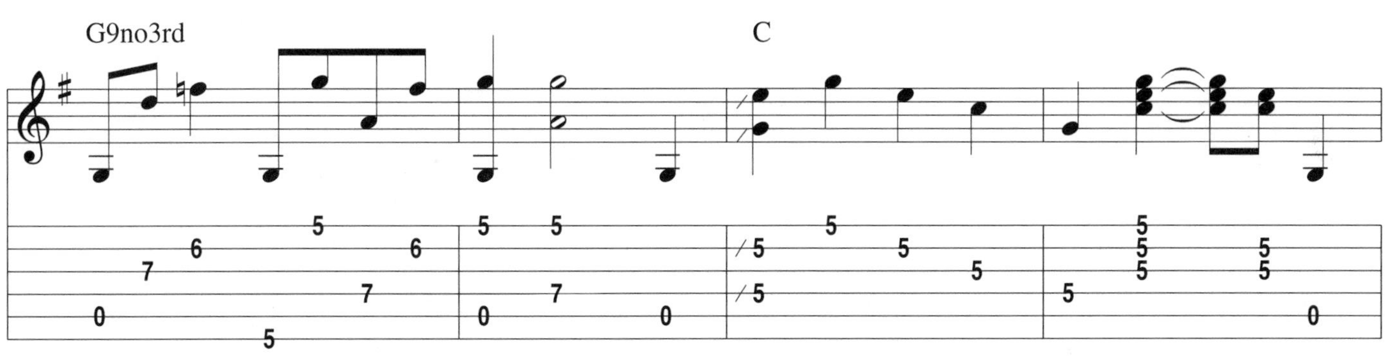
G9no3rd
C

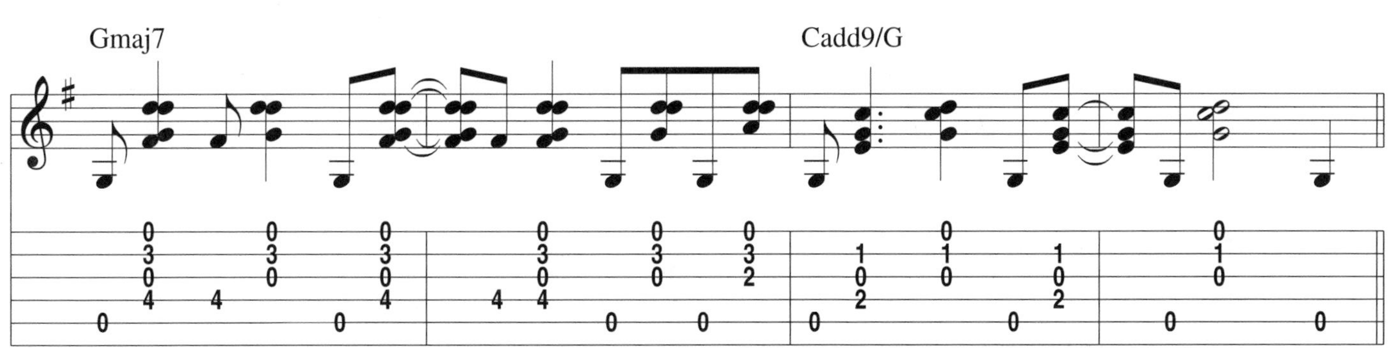
Gmaj7
Cadd9/G

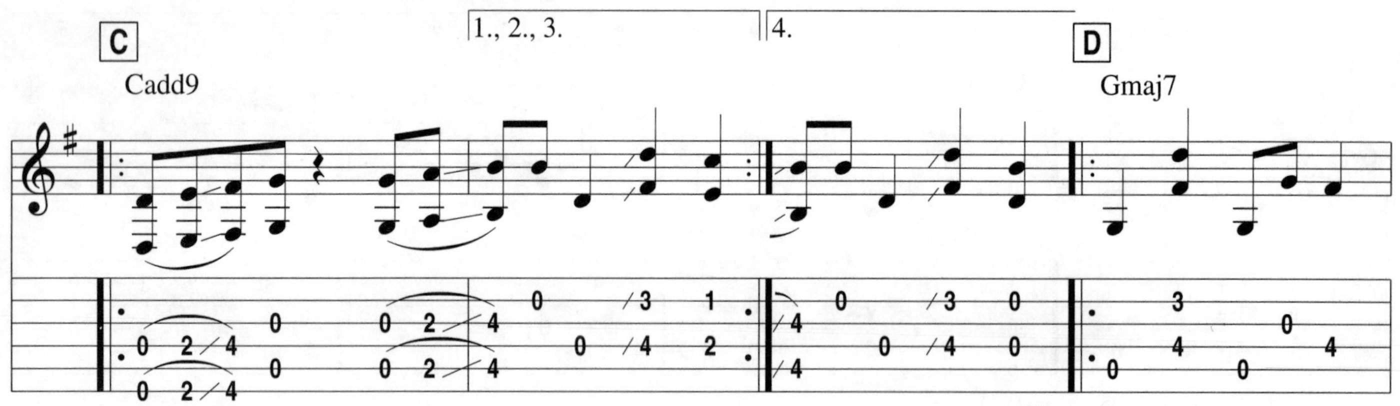
C
1., 2., 3.
4.
D
Cadd9
Gmaj7

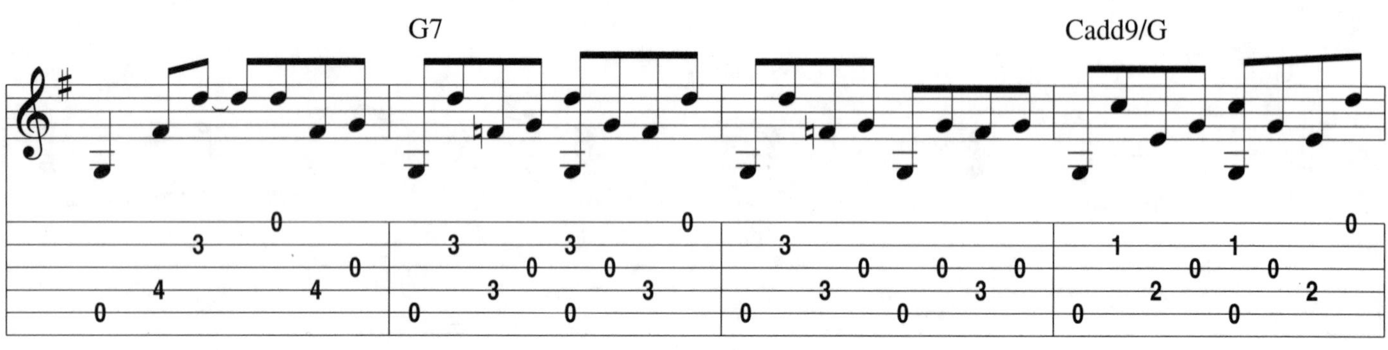
G7
Cadd9/G

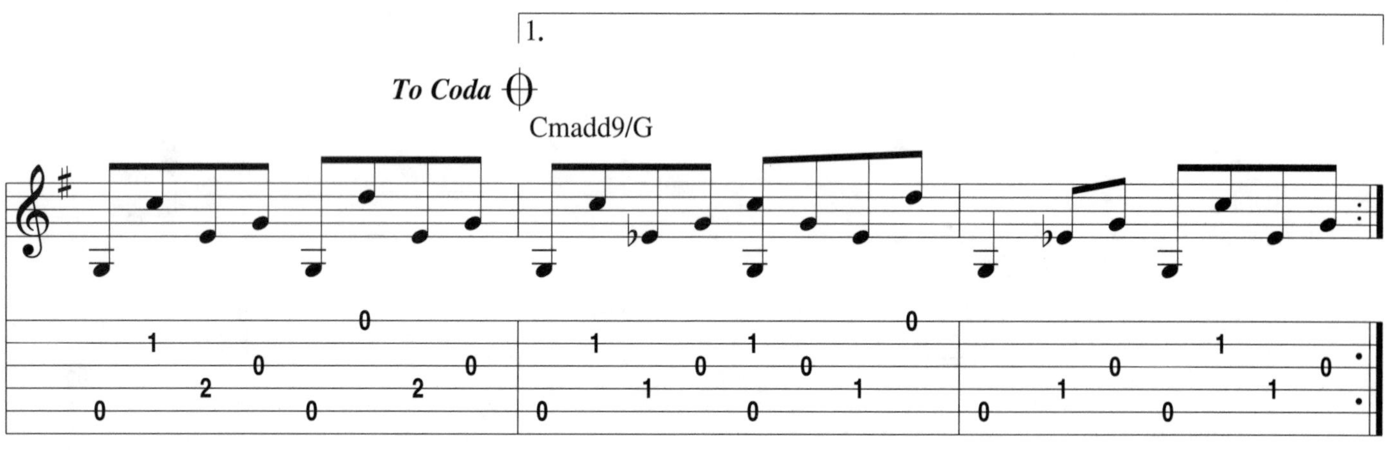
1.
To Coda
Cmadd9/G

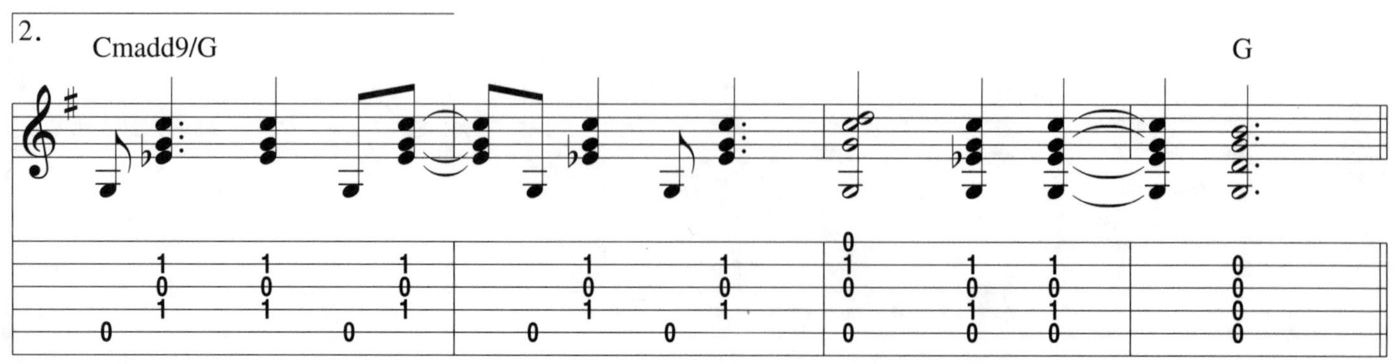
2.
Cmadd9/G
G

D. C., play entire form:
(A B C B1 C1 D E)
then ***D.C. al Coda***

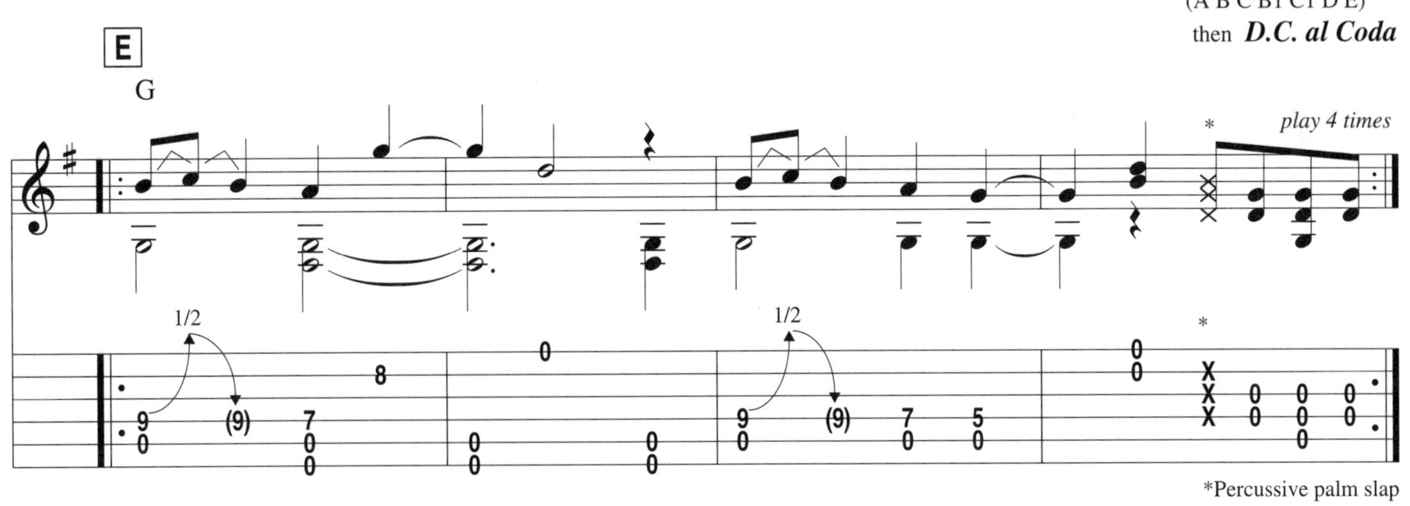

*Percussive palm slap

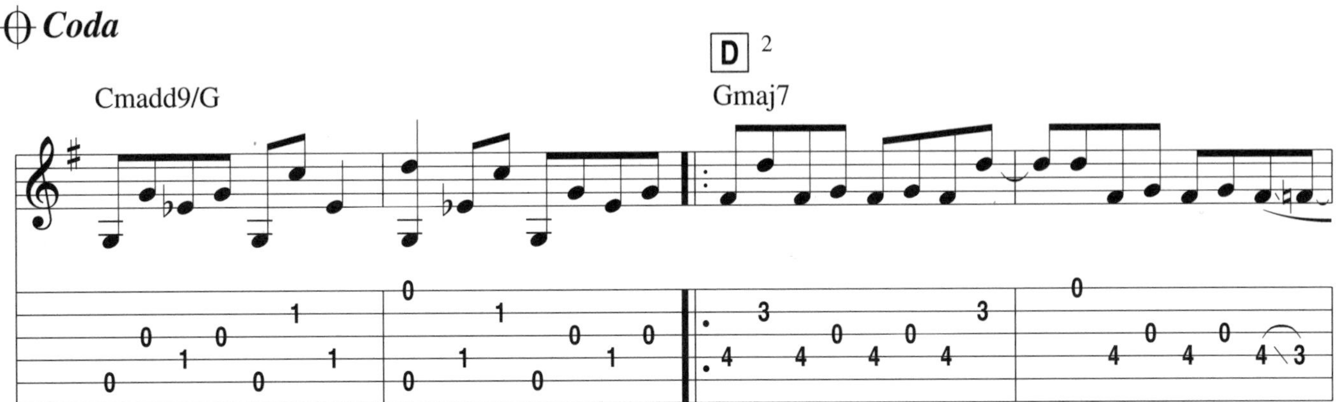

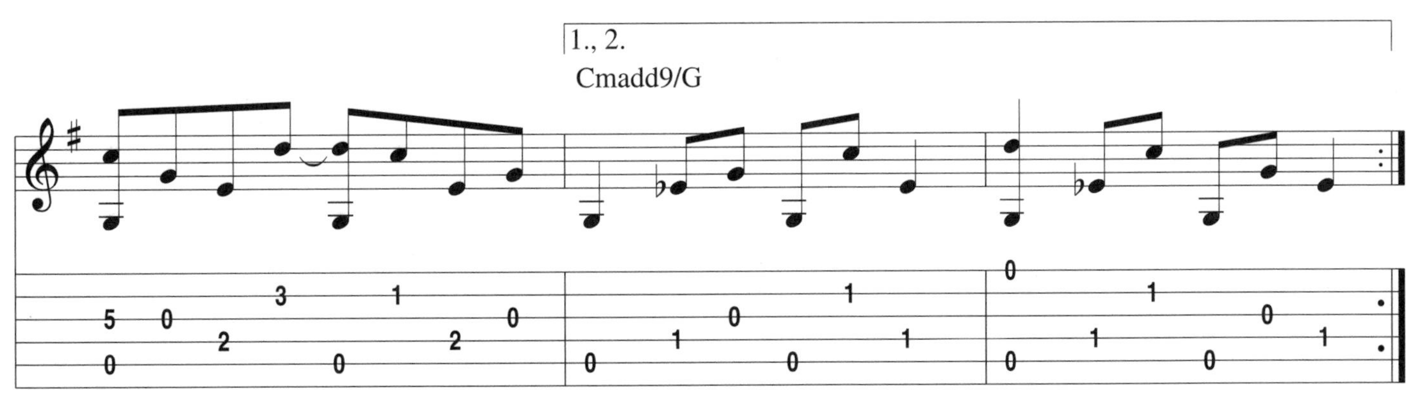

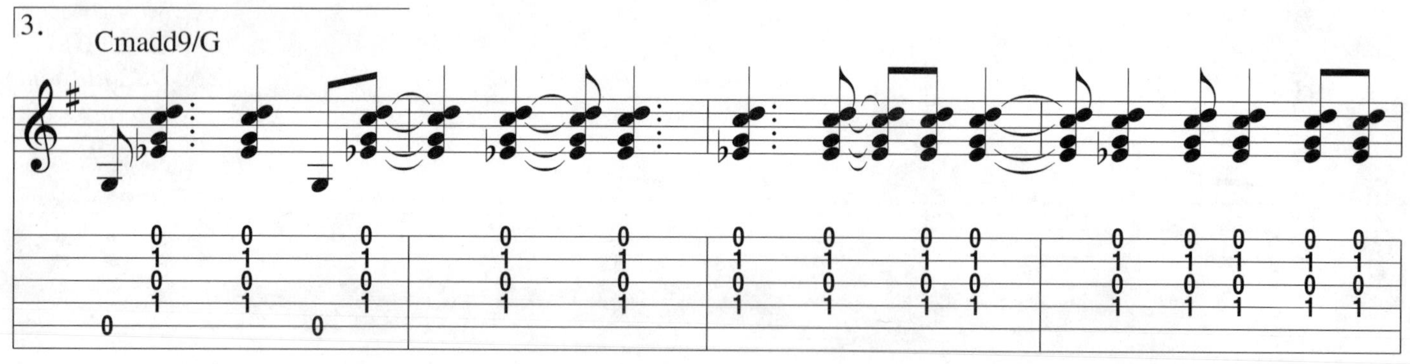
3.
Cmadd9/G

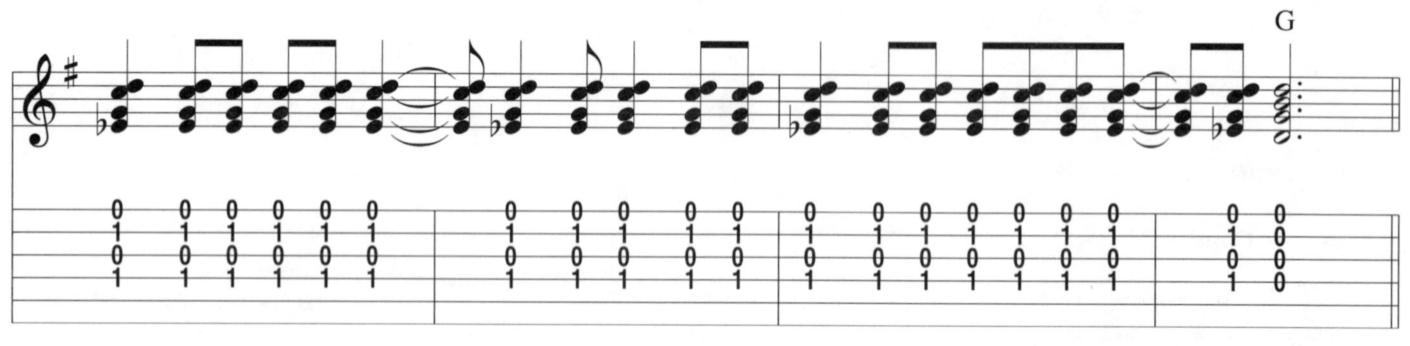
G

E 2
G
play 7 times
1/2
1/2

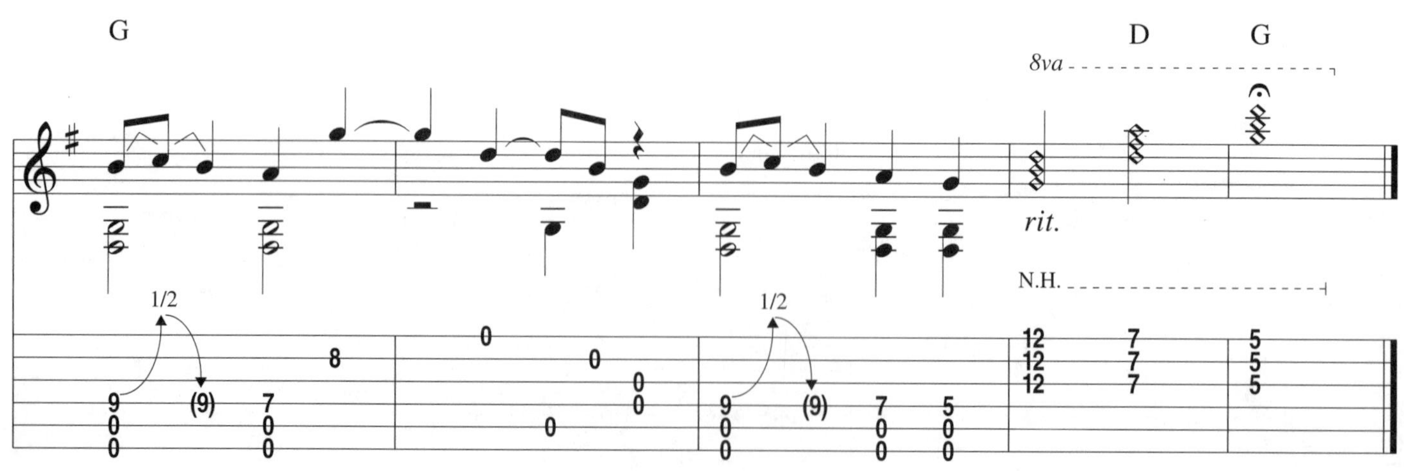
G
D
G
8va
rit.
N.H.
1/2
1/2

HOMESPUN®

LISTEN & LEARN SERIES

This exciting new series features lessons from the top pros with in-depth CD instruction and thorough accompanying book.

GUITAR

Russ Barenberg Teaches Twenty Bluegrass Guitar Solos

00695220 Book/CD Pack $19.95

Rory Block Teaches Classics of Country Blues Guitar
00699065 Book/CD Pack $19.95

Cathy Fink and Marcy Marxer's Kids' Guitar Songbook
00695258 Book/CD Pack $14.95

The Guitar of Jorma Kaukonen
00695184 Book/CD Pack $19.95

Tony Rice Teaches Bluegrass Guitar
00695045 Book/CD Pack $19.95

Artie Traum Teaches Essential Chords & Progressions for Acoustic Guitar
00695259 Book/CD Pack $14.95

Artie Traum Teaches 101 Plus Essential Riffs for Acoustic Guitar
00695260 Book/CD Pack $14.95

Happy Traum Teaches Blues Guitar
00841082 Book/CD Pack $19.95

Richard Thompson Teaches Traditional Guitar Instrumentals
00841083 Book/CD Pack $19.95

BANJO

Tony Trischka Teaches 20 Easy Banjo Solos
00699056 Book/CD Pack $19.95

PIANO

David Bennett Cohen Teaches Blues Piano
00841084 Volume 1 Book/CD Pack $19.95
00290498 Volume 2 Book/CD Pack $19.95

Warren Bernhardt Teaches Jazz Piano
Volume 1 – A Hands-On Course in Improvisation and Technique
00699062 Volume 1 Book/CD Pack $19.95
Volume 2 – Creating Harmony and Building Solos
00699084 Volume 2 Book/CD Pack $19.95

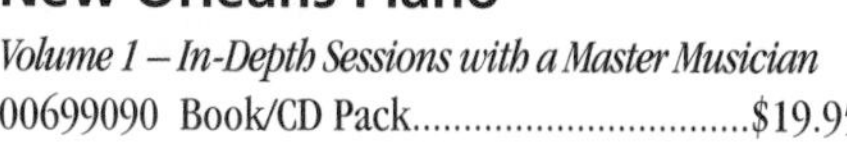
Dr. John Teaches New Orleans Piano
Volume 1 – In-Depth Sessions with a Master Musician
00699090 Book/CD Pack $19.95
Volume 2 – Building a Blues Repertoire
00699093 Book/CD Pack $19.95
Volume 3 – Sanctifying the Blues
00699094 Book/CD Pack $19.95

HARMONICA

Paul Butterfield Teaches Blues Harmonica
00699089 Book/CD Pack $19.95

John Sebastian Teaches Blues Harmonica
00841074 Book/CD Pack $19.95

PENNYWHISTLE

Cathal McConnell Teaches Irish Pennywhistle
00841081 Book/CD Pack $19.95

FOR MORE INFORMATION, SEE YOUR LOCAL MUSIC DEALER, OR WRITE TO:

HAL•LEONARD® CORPORATION
7777 W. BLUEMOUND RD. P.O. BOX 13819 MILWAUKEE, WI 53213

0198

Continue Your Studies With Jorma Kaukonen!

If you enjoyed this Listen & Learn Publication, you'll want to know about other terrific guitar instruction products by Jorma Kaukonen.

VIDEO LESSONS

The Acoustic Guitar Of Jorma Kaukonen
Blues, Rags and Originals

Video One - ***100 minutes***
with special guest Jack Casady

Jorma teaches his solid fingerpicking blues style through some of his favorite traditional and original tunes: *West Coast Blues, Hesitation Blues, Crystal City* and *Embryonic Journey*. Includes tips on picking style, slide technique, open tunings and a demonstration with Jefferson Airplane/Hot Tuna partner Jack Casady.

Video Two - ***90 minutes***

Jorma continues his examination of the blues-based fingerpicking that has long been his signature style. He takes apart some favorites from his repertoire, teaching the elements that make his arrangements so memorable. Songs include the folk/blues *I Know You Rider*, his original *Water Song* and the perennial favorite *San Francisco Bay Blues*.

Video Three - ***80 minutes***

Here Jorma applies his techniques to the traditional and original songs that he made famous, both as a solo artist and with Hot Tuna. This video will be a delight to all of Jorma's fans, as well as to lovers of acoustic blues and fingerpicking guitar. Songs include: *I Will Be All Right, Keep Your Lamp Trimmed and Burning, Been So Long, Ice Age, Mann's Fate, Third Week in the Chelsea* and *Ninety-Nine Year Blues.*

The Electric Guitar Of Jorma Kaukonen - ***90-minute video***
Blues, Rock 'n' Roll and Beyond
with special guests Electric Hot Tuna: Jack Casady (bass), Michael Falzarano (guitar) and Harvey Sorgen (drums)

A formula for instant success on the electric guitar! Jorma Kaukonen teaches licks, solos, lead lines and rhythm grooves to rival the best of them. Instructional and entertaining, Jorma and Electric Hot Tuna give powerful rock renditions of the songs taught: *Hit Single #1*, *Homespun Blues* and *Ode To Billy Dean.*

These and hundreds of other top instructional tapes are available from your music dealer or directly from Homespun Tapes. For complete catalog, write or call:

Box 340 • Woodstock, NY 12498 • (800) 33-TAPES • (914) 246-2550